The Magnetic Heart of God

Praise for *The Magnetic Heart of God*

Powerful ... Brilliant ... Captivating. *The Magnetic Heart of God* is a "must read" for everyone, whether they are agnostics, irreligious or believers in Christ. For Christians, The Magnetic Heart of God will bring fresh insights and application in our own walk with Christ and in discipling others.

Kamel H Shalhoub, The Navigators, Middle East North Africa (MENA), Regional Director Emeritus

I believe *The Magnetic Heart of God* to be the most pivotal work of spiritual literature produced in the twenty-first century. It magnifies the relevance of Christ on a level never before articulated. *The Magnetic Heart of God* is edgy, enlightening, comforting, and brilliantly crafted. I will read over and over again.

Raymond Reed, *The Independent*

If you have just stumbled onto Cory Rosenke's *The Magnetic Heart of God,* you have stumbled onto a gem. He has marvelously connected God's Scripture with our souls. Chapters 5, 6, and 7 better describe the human condition than any psychology textbook ever printed. If you ever experience feelings of loneliness, insecurity, or insignificance, or you know anyone who has, you can't go wrong by reading *The Magnetic Heart of God.* I recommend it to you.

Dr. Woodrow Kroll, president & senior Bible teacher (retired), Back to the Bible International

You're not simply holding a book, you're clutching a poignantly crafted resource that could change the way you understand you, your relationships, and even God Himself. *The Magnetic Heart of God* is a deep dive into both our humanity and God's divine nature, each chapter an eloquent glimpse into not only who we are but the why of who we are. And the latter is just what we need to embrace every good thing God intends for us in Christ.

Cortney Donelson, founder of vocem LLC and
award-winning author of several books, including
Clay Jar, Cracked: When We're Broken But Not Shattered

The Magnetic Heart of God is not a book you simply read and then set aside. It's a book you interact with. This isn't about religion; it's a book about living the abundant and blessed life that God fully intended for His people to experience in Christ. If you are ready for a significant boost in your spiritual life, your journey can begin by reading *The Magnetic Heart of God*.

J. Carl Laney, ThD, professor emeritus, Western Seminary

Cory Rosenke has gifted us a marvelous adventure through the human heart. He shows us the basic yearnings of what it means to be human and clearly demonstrates our fallen estate—and God's answers to raise us up. The power of the book is the way that Rosenke crafts a narrative to draw the reader into a story, then connect the dots between the human condition and the hope of the gospel. *The Magnetic Heart of God* is a solid read for those yearning to understand how the gospel is relevant to the issues of twenty-first-century life.

Rev. Dr. David Chotka, chair, Alliance Pray Canada
(C&MA Canada), author of *Hey! Are You There?*
It's Me—God, director of SpiritEquip Ministries

The Magnetic Heart of God will help you uncover the very heart of your personal unhappiness and provide powerful solutions resulting in a life of true abundance. Cory Rosenke not only makes difficult concepts simple, but he also provides practical pathways toward a hope and joy-filled lifestyle that reflects and proclaims the nature of a loving God.

Chuck Starnes, relationship coach

A friend of mine describes the gospel as divine abundance lavished on human need. It's the prodigal's story told over and over, for this one, and this one, and this one, world without end. All we have to do, as that first prodigal did, is "come to our senses," and then head home. I find that lovely. I also find, on that definition, Cory's book pure gospel: for he cannot stop speaking about, with joy and undimmed wonder, "Heavenly Provision," God's bread to spare for all that aches and wants in us. He is so wise, and gentle, in naming the thousand ways we mess this up, and keep going to the wrong well, keep ending up at the swine's trough. And he is such a gladsome herald of the true feast, and goes to all the highways and byways to makes sure we get invited. Don't miss your invitation.

Mark Buchanan, Author of *God Walk:*
Moving at the Speed of Your Soul

the MAGNETIC HEART *of* GOD

Understanding the
Five Cravings of Your Soul

CORY ROSENKE

NASHVILLE

NEW YORK • LONDON • MELBOURNE • VANCOUVER

the MAGNETIC HEART *of* GOD

Understanding the Five Cravings of Your Soul

Published in New York, New York, by Morgan James Publishing. Morgan James is a trademark of Morgan James, LLC. www.MorganJamesPublishing.com

Unless otherwise marked, Scripture taken from THE HOLY BIBLE, NEW INTERNATIONAL VERSION ®. Copyright©1973, 1978, 1984, 2011 by Biblica, Inc.™. Used by permission of Zondervan.

Scripture marked NLT are taken from the HOLY BIBLE, NEW LIVING TRANSLATION (NLT): Copyright©1996, 2004, 2007 by Tyndale House Foundation. Used by permission of Tyndale House Publishers, Inc., Carol Stream, Illinois 60188. All rights reserved. Used by permission.

Mere Christianity by C. S. Lewis © copyright C. S. Lewis Pte Ltd 1942, 1943, 1944, 1952. Extract used with permission.

Proudly distributed by Publishers Group West®

Morgan James BOGO™

A **FREE** ebook edition is available for you or a friend with the purchase of this print book.

_____

CLEARLY SIGN YOUR NAME ABOVE

Instructions to claim your free ebook edition:
1. Visit MorganJamesBOGO.com
2. Sign your name CLEARLY in the space above
3. Complete the form and submit a photo of this entire page
4. You or your friend can download the ebook to your preferred device

ISBN 9781636981826 paperback
ISBN 9781636981833 ebook
Library of Congress Control Number: 2023934890

Cover Design by:
Rachel Lopez
www.r2cdesign.com

Interior Design by:
Chris Treccani
www.3dogcreative.net

Morgan James PUBLISHING Builds *with...* **Habitat for Humanity® Peninsula and Greater Williamsburg**

Morgan James is a proud partner of Habitat for Humanity Peninsula and Greater Williamsburg. Partners in building since 2006.

Get involved today! Visit: www.morgan-james-publishing.com/giving-back

For all those who have ever wondered why . . .

Table of Contents

Preparing for the Journey

To begin with, I would like to thank you for opening the first few pages of this book. I feel a genuine rush of excitement as I consider the transformative journey you are about to embark upon. Self-discovery is an authentic, real-life adventure, a daring odyssey on which we explore the mysterious realm of our deepest selves. Buried treasure is uncovered, fears are confronted, and life-changing epiphany might lie waiting behind any bend in the trail. If courage, humility, and honesty are maintained, the intrepid traveler safely reemerges a more confident and complete person. Truly, self-discovery grows, strengthens, and expands us. Still, such *up-close* revelation can feel intimidating to some, as it alters not only the way we see ourselves but also the way we perceive everything around us. Like any good adventure, self-discovery *changes* the adventurer. I admire your willingness to pursue this elevated perspective, as many prefer to remain in a vulnerable state of naivety, and even oblivion. Sadly (as we will learn in upcoming chapters), such ignorance does *not* bring bliss. Far from it! Your courage to move forward suggests that you are ready for what you are about to experience next.

In the interest of preparedness, it seems prudent to share a few introductory words in the hope that they might better equip you for the upcoming venture. I'll begin by establishing my five-fold purpose so that you aren't left guessing as to my intentions.

In writing these pages, I have endeavored to accomplish nothing less than to

1. accurately diagnose our floundering personal and social condition,
2. reintroduce you to your soul in a fresh and transformational way,
3. clarify the true purpose and meaning of human existence,
4. carefully map out the most reliable route to abundant life, and
5. expand your perspective regarding God and His intentions toward you.

This adventure will weave through the origins of your ancient past, trek the hidden mysteries of a promised future, and boldly navigate the uncertainties of your personal now. Together, we will explore a previously undiscovered point of *convergence*: an existential plane where groundbreaking philosophy, sound theology, proven psychology, and universal experience cohesively unite to deliver a soul-stirring message that will beautifully transform the lives of any who are willing to receive it.

As you can see, my intentions are not small. In an effort to accomplish this gargantuan task, I will employ revealing personal testimony and allegorical stories. I'll attempt to disseminate a lifetime of exploratory research and study, even as we traverse the deep riches of God's Word, and follow the trail of breadcrumbs left by some of history's greatest thinkers.

G. K. Chesterton once said, "I have found only one religion which dares go down with me into the depths of myself."

I would pose his findings to be worthy of examination, and so we will look (with fresh and discerning eyes) toward the radical Person of Jesus.

In consideration of both my intended purpose and the epic route upon which this expedition will proceed, I encourage you to pace yourself. Take ample time as you read—there's no rush. Find a quiet corner with minimal distractions, grab yourself a snack and a beverage (maybe even a pencil or highlighter), wrap yourself in a cozy blanket, and begin exploring the marvelous and mysterious depths of your soul.

I wish you well in your valiant pursuit.

Part 1

THEN SINGS MY SOUL

Chapter 1

THE AGONY AND
THE ECSTASY

A warm summer breeze caressed a tear-stained cheek as the man in the blue shirt stepped toward the ledge of the high-rise rooftop. Overhead, the setting sun splashed marvelous beauty across the wide expanse of the evening sky. Tepid violet was merging into vibrant purple, and slowly, both shades were being drawn into the red-and-yellow flame of the horizon. Never before, even since the creation of the world, had this particular sky been witnessed. It was unique, dramatic, and breathtaking. Yet the man in the blue shirt took no notice. His focus was inward—and downward.

One step forward, *and fifty-two stories below*, lay the grim surface of the city street and possibly, just maybe, an end to the pain: a desperate and terrible solution to his confusion and despair. Unaware of the life-and-death struggle unfolding in their midst, the rooftop birds continued to chirp and flutter, engaged in an epic battle over old sesame seeds. The monotonous hum of traffic could be heard rising on the updraft, broken occasionally by an impatient car horn or the insistent bell of the commuter train. The world was ignorantly going about its business.

Alone on the ledge, precariously teetering between the majestic sky above and the harsh finality of the street below, the life in the blue shirt hung in the balance. Hope was besieged by despair, the hunger to feel, by the wish to feel no more.

How had it come to this?

The blue shirt had been a recent gift from his wife, given in celebration of his forty-fifth birthday. In fact, for each of their fifteen years of marriage, she had gifted him a new shirt on his big day. It had become a pleasant and anticipated tradition—yet this had been the last one, the last time. A few days earlier, over a quiet dinner together, his wife informed him she was leaving him, that she didn't love him anymore. She and their two children were going to stay with her sister in Los Angeles until divorce plans could be finalized. There was no bitterness or aggression in her tone, just the matter-of-fact styling of a long-rehearsed speech. She spoke softly, even covering his hand with her own as if to soften the blow. The impact of the announcement (and her subsequent departure) had been completely unexpected, and for the first few days, the emptiness of their big home hadn't seemed real to him. It was all just a terrible dream, one he was sure to awaken from. But he hadn't woken up. It was *real* now, and the pain was unbearable.

Forty-five years of sweat and struggle … and for what? What had any of it accomplished? He had done everything the world had asked him to do, and more. He had graduated high school, not at the top of his class, but not at the bottom, either. His gift was athletics, and it earned him a football scholarship to a highly coveted Ivy League university. Life had been rich with adventure and promise. Stadiums, fraternities, dorm-room parties. Throughout those hallowed years, he successfully juggled the pursuit of sports, sex, and higher education. Wasn't that supposed to be the kickoff to the American dream? The official template for happiness and success? He had proudly donned the school colors, and he graduated with a division championship, a Bachelor's Degree in Psychology, and a Master's in Business. These achievements were gained, even though his childhood had been marred by poverty, abuse, and uncertainty. Yet he had allowed nothing to hold him back. In the eyes of the world, his was an inspiring success story, a true rags-to-riches inspiration, and his office wall was adorned with enough trophies and plaques to prove it.

Purposefully, diligently, the man in the blue shirt had worked hard to ensure his own children would never have to experience the same early hardships that he himself had endured as a child. They would begin life on a firmer foundation, lacking nothing. That had been the plan ... but it had all fallen apart. His biggest fear had come true. He had somehow repeated the failure of his father, unwittingly loading a burden of heartache and confusion on the backs of his children. One thing they would not have to be concerned about was poverty, but that was a small consolation.

Finances were no longer an issue in the blue-shirt household. Upon graduating from university, he started his own company. Fueled by hard work and entrepreneurial genius, it had all come together at the right time and in the right place. Business was booming, and his company was thriving, even receiving international acclaim. Over the past decade, his name had become synonymous with growth, profit, stability, and ingenuity. With the trappings of well-earned success, he had purchased several beautiful homes, each in relation to an early childhood wish list: a beach house, a country getaway, and a downtown penthouse. His family regularly enjoyed vacations in Hawaii, Italy, France, and countless other coveted destinations ... but it was all meaningless! *It had all been for nothing!*

Even before his wife's devastating departure, the sparkle of wealth had begun to fade, being replaced by an unwelcome, yet ever-intensifying, sense of emptiness. While lavish comfort was firmly within his grasp, peace and happiness had remained elusive. Of course, he had experienced *moments* of peace, even seasons of happiness, but they were generally associated with a happening of some sort: a celebration, a holiday, an achievement—all of which were unsustainable, all of which came to an inevitable end. In the post-happening quiet, a disturbing sense of emptiness would again take hold. For years, he had fought back with determination, seeking to reignite his excitement, his passion, his purpose. He started *more* companies, made *bigger* investments, planned even more lavish social gatherings; but with each passing achievement, the emptiness seemed only to grow.

At times, he longed for the naivety and even the poverty of his youth. He remembered with great fondness those early days when the promise of success and achievement still filled him with a thrilling sense of purpose. Now he *was* a success, having achieved even beyond his wildest dreams ... but the promise had been a lie! Like the legions of wealthy people before him, he now knew the words of Jack Higgins to be true: "When you get to the top, there's nothing there." Instead of peace and happiness, all he discovered were fresh disappointments, new lives and possessions to covet, a higher level of stress, and the same old relational conflicts.

Two years ago, he had begun looking for solace in a bottle. It hadn't worked. Like every other high, it too would dissipate, replacing itself not only with a sense of emptiness but also with deep shame.

It was all meaningless! His hard work, his education, his wealth—all meaningless! He possessed everything the world had to offer, and it wasn't enough. Pain and confusion coursed through him. *He loved her* … he had such great hopes for his kids … if only …

As the light in the sky continued to fade, the man in the blue shirt looked down at the twinkle of human life bustling below him. Damp with tears, a slow, sardonic smile formed at the corner of his lips as he whispered, "What would my parents, my professors, my employees, or my wife think if they could see how pathetic I—" His musings were cut short as he was suddenly struck by a violent jolt. He lost his balance, and the world began to spin.

THE PROBLEM

Before we move forward, I would like to invite you to pause and reflect on the above story. My intent has not been to trigger or manipulate you through the telling of a dramatic tale. Rather, my hope has been to engage you in an honest moment. Sadly, *the man in the blue shirt* is emblematic of many tragic scenarios unfolding throughout our world today—even at this precise moment. And while I leave it to your imagination to determine the story's ending, the discouragement, confusion, and despair we witness throughout every level of society, even one as rich and well-educated as our own, is not something we need leave to the imagination. The tragic evidence is all around us, evocative and all too real. It exists in the high-rise office buildings, even as it exists in the homeless encampments. To varying degrees, a similar sense of emptiness may be lurking (and possibly even growing) within the privacy of your own heart. Clearly, not everyone will end up on a rooftop. Still, the hard truth is, as Henry David Thoreau pointed out, "The mass of men lead lives of quiet desperation."

We have a problem. We live in a time of unprecedented prosperity, and yet the measure of our collective emptiness is also unprecedented. Never before has such an abundance of opportunity, selection, and leisure been so readily available to so many people ... yet we remain largely unfulfilled. As a result, the earth is now laced with the paths of prosperous and educated multitudes, all wandering to and fro on a desperate quest to discover hope and meaning. All this despite an ever-increasing collection of freedoms and conveniences.

How is this even possible?

Without truly understanding *why* the problem exists, yet sensing the urgent nature of the issue, the world has rushed to pose its predictable solutions to the problem. If you have ever sat in a university classroom, watched a television commercial, listened to a motivational speaker, or scrolled through social media content, you have no doubt heard these proposed solutions loud and clear. Essentially, the world has doubled down on its original misdiagnosis, merely prescribing higher and higher dosages of the same failed medication: wealth, power, fame, freedom, education, sex, and self-care. Yet the problem stubbornly remains and even expands. The plot thickens as we realize this is not merely a secular issue. Many Christians have also felt the unwelcome presence of emptiness and discouragement, even after sitting through countless sermons on the goodness and greatness of God.

So what do we do about it? This is clearly a global dilemma! How do we address it? What strategy will prove most effective?

Before we can accurately answer these *what* and *how* questions, we must first uncover the root of our mysterious *why*. We need to identify the *source* of the problem. For example, my finger hurts! *Why* does my finger hurt? Did I hit it with a hammer? Did I burn it in hot water? That's not it. I see the problem now—there's a big thorn sticking out of it! This is important information, as we do not treat a puncture wound in the same manner we treat a burn or break. The diagnosis must be accurate, or the prescription will prove ineffective, possibly even detrimental. In the case of our human emptiness, unfulfillment,

A PRIMARY GOAL OF THIS BOOK IS TO REMOVE THE MASK AND NAME NAMES.

and increasing agitation, discovering the *why* will require a deep dive into the secret *motives* and *ambitions* of the human soul, motives and ambitions with which many have lived and loved unaware. These twin stimulants, these covert influencers, have lingered in the shadows of our consciousness, ever in the peripheral, active and insistent, but masked and unnamed. A primary goal of this book is to remove the mask and name names. We have remained a mystery to ourselves for far too long. The soul within us has an important story to tell, and we would benefit greatly by listening. As you tune your ear to hear its voice, you will become privy to information (and possibly even scandal) about which you were previously uninformed: the veiled truth about your neighbor, the hidden ambitions of your government representative, the enigmas that are your spouse—and *yourself*. By finally divulging these well-kept secrets, we will neither violate nor betray; rather, bringing them to light will enhance and empower us all.

David sang to God in Psalm 139:14, declaring, "I praise you, because I am fearfully and wonderfully made."

So are you, to a deeper degree than you have likely imagined. We are biological beings, compiled of flesh, and heavily influenced by brain and body chemicals: neurons, cells, hormones, DNA, and countless miles of micro-corridors connecting them all together.

Yet we are also spiritual beings, equipped with an eternal soul and possessing a level of consciousness that reaches far beyond the borders of mere biology. You are wonderfully made, and your soul has been longing to tell you all about it. It's time to pause and listen.

WONDERFULLY MADE

Every epic tale begins with an informative backstory that strengthens our connection with the main characters. The story of your soul deserves nothing less, so I begin at the beginning. If you are a current subscriber to Charles Darwin and his famed theory, rest assured, I won't spend my energy incessantly trying to dissuade you otherwise. There are many fine books specifically written to facilitate such a discussion, and I would direct you toward them. Instead, I will simply share what I believe to be true of our beginnings.

Scripture explicitly teaches that we are created in the image of God.

> *So God created mankind in his own image,*
> *in the image of God he created them;*
> *male and female he created them* (Genesis 1:27).

It is important that we allow the magnitude of this statement to fully wash over us. It exposes a vast and irreconcilable contrast between creation and evolution, one that finds divergence, not simply on the issue of first cause, but regarding intended design as well. The theory of evolution suggests a biological design evolved solely for the purpose of earthly survival. Comparatively, to be made in the image of God marks humanity with bold and transcendent distinction. While each component of creation can boast of intricate design and unique beauty, mankind alone was created in God's image and filled with His breath. This is the heritage of our bodies, minds, and souls. The impact of this reality greatly affects how we see ourselves, and how we see ourselves will impact everything else.

Another contrast between creation and evolution is that of purpose. Evolution suggests no objective apart from survival, with existence itself being the result of random happenstance. Scripture, however, paints a very different picture. With each stroke of the doctrinal brush, the portrait takes shape, and a great and glorious purpose is revealed: God created mankind with an exclusive privilege, namely, to *know* Him and to experience the joy of being known *by* Him. Or, as the acclaimed catechism states, "The chief end of man is to glorify God and enjoy Him forever."

Merely eking out an existence amid the dirt and the asphalt was not, and is not, our intended destiny. We have been made for something more. Your soul wants you to know this!

As with many important topics, A. W. Tozer masterfully describes what it means to be created in the image of God in a way that is not only true but also extremely clarifying and helpful. In his famed book, *The Pursuit of God*, he writes,

> *Being made in His image, we have within us the capacity to know Him. The moment the Spirit has quickened us to life in regeneration, our whole being senses its kinship to God and leaps up in joyous recognition. That is the heavenly birth without which we cannot see the kingdom of God. It is, however, not an end but an inception, for now begins the glorious pursuit, the heart's happy exploration of the infinite riches of the Godhead.*

In a nutshell, the Bible teaches this: that you (yes, I mean *you,* specifically) were created with both the unique capacity and the joyous purpose of living in happy communion with the Sovereign of the universe. What a privilege! What an adventure! What a delight! This happy communion is God's express desire for each one of us, and to this glorious end, He has woven into every human soul *five insatiable cravings,* cravings intentionally designed to propel us toward a relational connection with our Maker. These cravings will lead us to abundant life: purpose, fulfillment, and peace. Alternatively, if they are misdirected, these same cravings will condemn us to an existence rent with toil, struggle, hollow thrills, and the deep bitterness of unfulfilled desire. It is these five yearnings of the soul that I intend to explore with you. They are cravings felt both in the biological *and* the spiritual, yet sourced in the eternal. My express purpose is to cut through the fog of both modern philosophy and shallow religion, revealing an existential reality that has been hiding in plain sight, one that will help make sense of the chaos both without and within.

The human journey has never been easy, not since the mishap in the Garden of Eden; but it is greatly simplified when we understand where we came from, what it is we are truly looking for, and *why.*

Let's begin.

Chapter 2
THE DEEP WHY

The memory will always be precious to me. My three-year-old daughter and I were snuggling together on the couch, watching the classic VeggieTales episode "Rack, Shack, and Benny" for what must've been the hundredth time. Her tiny body leaned limp as a wet noodle against my chest, and she was almost asleep—*almost*. It was 8:30 p.m., and for the past twenty minutes, she had been fighting a valiant battle against sleepy eyelids. She was losing, but she wasn't yet ready to surrender. Periodically, her eyes would close, and her little blond head would slowly droop to the left. Just when I thought it was over, she would jerk back awake, staring with fresh determination at the television screen. She was a fighter, and she had been from the day of her birth. Still, she was going to lose this particular battle. Sleepy eyelids always win out in the end; it was only a matter of time.

The "Silly Songs with Larry" portion of the show had just ended, and she hadn't even flinched. That was the clear sign. She was asleep, and I was happy. As much as I enjoyed snuggling with my little girl, at times, it resembled cuddling a heated oven, and I needed some personal space to cool off. Cautiously, I reached for the remote. I glanced down. Her eyes were closed. Her breathing was soft and deep. It was time.

Ever so slowly, I sat up.

She jerked awake, twisting her head to look up at me with sleepy blue eyes. "Why did you turn off the TV, Daddy?" Her tone was slightly accusatory.

"Because it's bedtime, sweetheart." I sighed.

"Why, Daddy?"

Uh-oh! There it was. My knowledge of the universe was about to be tested by a thousand clever questions. Determined to prove myself, I answered, "Because if you don't go to sleep now, you'll be tired tomorrow. Then you'll be grumpy at Grandma's."

"Why, Daddy?"

"Because our bodies need to get lots of rest, or they don't work properly. Mommy and I need to go to bed soon too."

She looked at me for a moment, as if considering what I had just said. Then she asked, "Why, Daddy?"

Throughout the remainder of our bedtime routine, I was besieged with the same persistent question, and each answer seemed only to inspire new curiosity. Before I knew it, we had covered topics ranging from Grandma's health and song lyrics to the comforting nature of teddy bears. Eventually, I would have to get tough and repeat the same tired line I had heard from my parents: "It's time to stop talking and go to sleep!"

This is what bedtime sounded like in our household.

THE UNIVERSAL WHY

Chances are you have been involved in a similar line of questioning. From an early age, we intuitively ask the all-important question of *why*, and our want for an answer will end only in the glories of heaven. This question will remain on the tip of our tongues throughout the entirety of our earthly lives: a top priority, perhaps even growing more insistent with age. We ask this question to make sense *of* and feel safe *in* the world around us. To that important end, imagine if you possessed the insight to look around you and truly understand *why* people do what they do, why they desire the things they desire, say the things they say, and behave the way they behave. Or perhaps even more exciting—imagine if you had the discernment to look *within yourself* and truly understand why *you* feel the way you feel, why you are responding to a given situation the way you are. They say knowledge is power, and that statement is definitely true in this instance.

Aristotle is attributed with saying, "Knowing yourself is the beginning of all wisdom."

That is a bold supposition, but from a social science perspective (and most definitely a psychological one), I believe he was on to something. Comprehending "why I do what I do" is often the first step toward making sense of our chaos, and it is therefore the first step toward growth and solution.

Imagine if you could finally understand why your coworker belittles the people around him, why your spouse gets so defensive, or why you feel strangely unfulfilled in what you thought would be a meaningful career or relationship.

At a shallow glance, the *why* may appear obvious. Perhaps you presume that someone merely "fell out of love" or that your job just "isn't a good fit for you anymore." But why did the feelings change? What were you looking for when you entered the relationship in the first place? And what have you *not found* that is currently prompting you to detach and look elsewhere? Learning to identify the deeper desire lurking beneath the surface will empower you to respond to life's ebb and flow with more effect. It will also enhance your ability to be a positive influence on the world around you.

Why did your neighbor run off on their spouse? *Why really?* Why won't my sister talk to me? *Why really?* Why does the world seem obsessed with money and sex? Why is everyone staring at their smartphones?

When we understand the *deep why*, we grow in our ability (and even our willingness) to respond with compassion, patience, tolerance, and *real solutions*. Such a perceptive response would greatly benefit everyone, including ourselves. So let's get to it. Let's uncover the mystery that is you and I.

THE ROLE OF THE SOUL

The comedic drama *O Brother, Where Art Thou* includes the story of a young man who sells his soul to the Devil in exchange for special musical abilities. When confronted with the potential consequences of his decision, the young man justifies the transaction by claiming of his soul, "I wasn't using it." While this story is clearly intended to be viewed as satire, it nonetheless exposes an extremely common misconception.

It would be a mistake to believe that your soul is mute or passive, that it is merely a fragile passenger, tethered to the flesh and along for the ride. Nothing could be farther from the truth. Frankly, the *opposite* is our reality. Our souls are bold, insistent, and alive with desire. When it comes to the trifecta of our being (our bodies, minds, and souls), it is our soul that is the alpha. It's the boss. It sends directives to the mind and the mind to the body. This is our internal chain of command. It is the hierarchy behind all other human hierarchies. Beyond our physical anatomy and mental acuity, *we are eternal souls!* This is the undying attribute that truly defines us! Everything changes the moment we authentically embrace this actuality.

At times, you'll hear someone say, "Follow your heart," or they will praise "the triumph of the human spirit." What they are referencing, perhaps without even knowing it, is the human soul. They are unofficially acknowledging the reality of a nonbiological presence, one that wields more influence than muscle, neural pathway, or nervous system. A great and life-changing self-awareness is experienced when we *officially* acknowledge the role of the soul, for therein, we finally identify the true source of our motivations. The biggest decisions we make in life do not originate in the brain or the body. The command is issued from a far deeper source.

I mentioned in the previous chapter that we are made in the image of God. By no means did I mean to insinuate that God, like us, runs about on two legs. Of course not. Rather, the image of God is molded into the larger, more encompassing essence of our being: *the soul.* This is the invisible part of us that Tozer pointed out, "Leaps up in joyous recognition" when it finally awakens to the presence of its Maker. It senses in God both its heritage and home.

God is to the soul what the round hole is to the round peg, the ocean to the dolphin, or the sky to the eagle. Apart from a connection with God, the human soul is hopelessly lost in a land of square holes. It gasps in distress like a fish out of water or scrambles in fear like a bird with clipped wings. This is the sad scenario currently raging beneath the fabric of our carefully airbrushed society. Having fooled ourselves into believing we are self-sufficient creatures, we have attempted to sever any reliance upon God. This unnatural rending has created a foreign and toxic environment, triggering a migration crisis of displaced souls. Billions now roam to and fro like hungry, disorientated, and increasingly irritable scavengers. They seek nourishment and fulfillment, but they find nothing on earth to satisfy their inner hunger. While the modern body is often pampered and well-fed and the mind highly stimulated, the souls of mankind have grown gaunt and desperate. When not rummaging about in search of relaxant or titillation, they perch defensively on an ever-increasing pile of earthly possessions … and starve.

A DESPERATE HUNGER

If you release a cow into a man-made paddock that is rich with grass and water, that cow will thrive. It will grow fat and happy, enjoying a peaceful existence. If you remove the cow and release a lion into that same paddock, the lion will soon become stressed. After thoroughly searching the enclosed area and finding nothing substantial to eat, the lion would likely begin looking for insects in the grass: worms, ants, and beetles. As it continues to search for food (or a way of escape), it would probably begin digging large holes. In desperation, it may even try eating the grass, but the grass won't satisfy a hungry lion. It would stare longingly at the birds flying overhead, perhaps even leaping toward the sky in impressive yet futile bounds. With both a loud roar and a soft growl, I imagine it would call out for help. Sadly, inevitably, as the terrible effects of starvation reach their peak, the lion would become weak and immobile. It would lie down in the rich green grass and die a hungry, cruel, and lonely death.

The world without God is this man-made paddock. The human soul is not the cow; *it is the lion.* The lesson we draw from the analogy is this: while the bounty of the earth can fully satisfy the needs of other living creatures, *it was not designed to satisfy the needs of the human soul.* For that, we must walk with God.

Contrary to the musings of some, you are not just another mammal. While monkeys may be happy with bananas and seagulls with whatever scraps they can find, we humans require more. Our needs are not many, but they differ substantially from the rest of creation. For far too long, we have treated ourselves like animals. We have given nourishment to the body and stimulation to the mind, but we have neglected our soul: the image of God, the core of who we are.

So what do you feed a hungry soul? What nourishment does it require? In answering these questions, we will open a whole new world of self-discovery.

NAMING NAMES

The soul within you experiences five core cravings. Even now, they are prompting and pulling you. These cravings did not evolve into being nor can they devolve out of being, for our Maker created them with intention and purpose. Throughout this book, I will refer to these collective cravings by an assortment of different names, *the cravings of the soul,* or by a slightly more academic title, *the five core humanities.* At other times, I will simply use its acronym, the FCH. We call them "humanities" for they effectively define the root of all human desire. They are the *deep why.*

Your soul will experience the pull of these cravings desperately and daily. They are at the very center of what it means to be human. These five hardwired, instinctive, insatiable cravings of the soul have driven every person in history to do everything we've ever done—

every member of every culture, of every ethnicity and every world-view, every gender and generation, all of humanity driven and propelled through life and time by the same five innate motivators:

SECURITY
IDENTITY
INDEPENDENCE
SIGNIFICANCE
INNOCENCE

These five words embody the dominant pentagram of all human ambition. Truly, the satisfaction of these five cravings is what we are hoping to experience in every human pursuit, every relationship we enter, every adventure we embark upon, and every utopia we attempt to build.

These five cravings are the itch your soul is seeking to scratch. If someone or something offers you security, identity, independence, significance, or innocence, you will want to engage with that person or thing. Conversely, if you perceive that someone or something is *threatening* your security, identity, independence, significance, or innocence, you will quickly avoid that person or thing. Subsequently, these cravings are the motivating force behind both marriage *and* divorce! They are the reason many of us feel a close connection to our family members—and why others haven't spoken to certain relatives in years. Realistically, or unrealistically, we enter every relationship with the implicit expectation that it will serve to enhance and protect our sense of security, identity, independence, significance, and innocence. And on the day we determine (fairly or unfairly) that certain relationships are falling short of this expectation, we will feel a strong urge to detach and withdraw.

War, romance, governance, industry, exploration—as real as gravity, the five core humanities impact every human movement. Truly, they are all-consuming! Consider these questions:

- What are we hoping to gain in the acquisition of wealth and possession?
- What are we hoping to manage through societal laws or protect with a well-equipped military?
- What are we hoping to experience in the pursuit of love, education, career, or achievement?

The answer to each of these questions is the same:

SECURITY—IDENTITY—INDEPENDENCE— SIGNIFICANCE—INNOCENCE

We can even observe the fingerprints of the five core humanities in the development of human morality. For example, those whom society has deemed to be "good people" are those who safeguard the core humanities of other people. These "good Samaritans" stand against injustice, defend the powerless, and actively give back to the community. They donate their time and resources to impactful organizations like Habitat for Humanity, Samaritan's Purse, or Saint Jude. They become our everyday heroes—and our comic book superheroes. Meanwhile, those deemed to be "bad people" are those we suspect of stealing or molesting the security, identity, independence, significance, or innocence of someone else. Both in real life and in fictional literature, these defilers are considered to be the villains. They cheat, threaten, oppress, and abuse the people around them in the selfish pursuit of their own profit and pleasure.

The metric is simple: good people *protect* and *share* the FCH while bad people attempt to *manipulate* and *monopolize* the FCH.

UNITY WITHIN DIVERSITY

We actively experience these cravings everywhere and in everything. They give a clear definition to our deepest *why*. In one moment, they may appear to be in direct conflict with each other (e.g., my craving for independence conceivably endangering my security or my aggressive pursuit of significance potentially jeopardizing my innocence) while in the next, they are blended together like the colors of a beautiful sunset, and it's hard to determine where one craving begins and the other ends.

Because of the vast measure of diversity inherent within our varied cultures, traditions, and life experiences, we may choose to seek satisfaction for our core humanities in very different places; nonetheless, it is the *same* selection of desires that motivates each one of us. For example, Tony may pursue significance through athletics, evaluating both himself and the people around him using a stopwatch and a weigh scale as his primary methods for measuring success. Tony is keenly interested in how fast and far you can run or how many pounds you can bench-press or squat. He may even awkwardly inquire as to your BMI. Meanwhile, Robert gives no thought to such interests. Instead, Robert measures significance through certificates and diplomas. Rob wants to know your GPA, which university you went to, and with what educational credential you graduated. He then ranks the people around him in accordance with that narrow metric. *Both* Tony and Robert are craving significance, but they've chosen to pursue fulfillment in differing sources.

Similarly, Mary may cling to the identity of her family name, taking great delight in her ancestry and genealogy. Mary is "daddy's little princess," and she proudly wears a T-shirt with that very phrase printed in bold type across the front. Conversely, Sophia's family experience was tragic, and the ensuing pain prompted her to place as much distance between herself and her relatives as possible. In lieu of her biological family, Sophia has pursued identity in relation to a specific social group, one that befriended her during a season of extreme vulnerability. Once again, both Mary and Sophia are driven by the same inner hunger for identity, but in opposing directions.

Finally, consider Sam and Annette. Sam feels most secure when someone else takes the lead, as it affords him the opportunity to fade safely into the background. Ever since he was very little, Sam has pursued security in anonymity and invisibility. Meanwhile, Annette doesn't feel secure unless she is up-front and in complete control. Some people appreciate her take-charge attitude, while others accuse her of being bossy or even power-hungry. (Interestingly, both Sam and Annette grew up in volatile homes, yet they developed contrasting styles of coping.)

For each of the individuals referenced, their varied environmental factors (and contrasting personal choices) resulted in the development of differing methods of pursuit. Nonetheless, it is the *same* collection of cravings prompting each of them.

> *(Side note: The primary mandates of a good counselor or therapist are to facilitate the healing of inner wounds and to aid in the development of healthier pursuit methods.)*

DEEPER STILL

Our core humanities reign as chief above any other human trait, and the influence they wield over every aspect of our daily lives cannot be overstated. They are the tie that binds philosophy, biology, anthropology, epistemology, physiology, theology, sociology, psychology, and virtually any other "ology" together. Truly, the study of anything "mankind related" ought to begin by considering the cravings of the soul. Finally awakening to this existential reality is both enlightening and empowering. If managed properly, this self and social awareness can yield great benefits, granting life-changing epiphany regarding the inner workings of both ourselves and the people around us. This fresh intuition allows us to become better spouses, friends, neighbors, and citizens. Still, there is an even deeper awareness yet to be explored, but gaining access to this chasmic level of consciousness requires that we navigate another batch of *what* and *why* questions. Questions like:

- *Why* do our souls have cravings?
- Now that we've acknowledged their all-consuming presence, *what* do they want from us?
- Why do they push and prod us as they do?
- What is their endgame?

These are crucial queries to investigate, as the most pivotal of all self-discoveries remain hidden within their answers.

In the case of our *physical* bodies, we know that our craving for food and water was specifically designed to motivate us *toward* something. We'll say things like "My stomach is growling" or "I feel parched," and these cravings then propel us toward actually consuming life-giving nutrients. Even in this basic biological sense, we discover ourselves to be fascinating creations. Just think of it: if we didn't experience the simple craving known as *thirst*, we wouldn't be reminded to consume water. And if we stopped drinking water, we would die of dehydration in less than a week! Clearly, how we choose to interact with our cravings will play a leading role in our overall health. So again we ask, *what purpose lies behind the cravings of our soul?* The answer to this question is both encouraging and profound!

Imagine God as a magnet and the craving of your soul as a molded piece of iron. The iron was *purposefully designed* to be drawn to the magnet. You are created in God's image, and as such, your soul feels the pull of His mighty heart.

Or let's look at it another way. Consider the migration instinct observed in certain birds or butterflies that miraculously traverse vast continents to reach a summer or winter haven or of sea turtles, which intuitively perambulate deep and wide oceans. Similarly, God placed the FCH in the human soul to help navigate a great spiritual migration, one specifically designed to draw us toward the safe harbor of a relationship with Him. No matter how far we may wander, we are each gifted with this internal compass: an innate longing, a purposeful hunger, lovingly designed to guide us safely home.

> YOU ARE CREATED IN GOD'S IMAGE, AND AS SUCH, YOUR SOUL FEELS THE PULL OF HIS MIGHTY HEART.

What an encouraging and momentous revelation! Security, identity, independence, significance, and innocence—these are not worldly cravings. They're *eternal* cravings—they're *Divine* cravings! This is a pivotal and self-revolutionary discovery, but it is tied to an important caution. The caution is this: if we don't recognize these Divine cravings for what they are, we will inevitably redirect them toward lesser nouns—temporal people, places, and things that cannot deliver satisfaction! The result will be an emptiness, a personal desperation, and a frustrating inability to experience lasting fulfillment, even amid an ever-increasing collection of earthly indulgences.

Sadly, it is the terrible effects of this disastrous misdirection that we see venting throughout much of the world today. Not surprisingly, it has given rise to an expanding fog of depression, confusion, and agitation—potentially at your own address.

Throughout the remainder of this book, we will explore each of these cravings on a deep and personal level, even mapping out the empty wasteland into which they are so often misdirected. We will continue to gather empirical, physical, and scriptural evidence, meticulously testing, fortifying, and expanding our belief systems. Additionally, we will celebrate the magnetic heart of God, that happy lure that never releases its faithful hold upon us no matter how dark and desperate things become. My overarching hope is that the skeptic will discover meaningful answers to his or her questions, that the wanderer will rediscover the path to abundant life, that the Christ follower will gain even greater confidence, and that the theologian, the counselor, and the scholar, will each glean a transformative insight.

As the awareness of our core humanities grows, we will uncover a previously hidden unity in the midst of our obvious diversity. This fresh awareness will, if we let it, increase our capacity for compassion, patience, tolerance, and *faith*. It will awaken a game-changing self-awareness, one that can greatly increase the quality of our everyday living. But of even higher value, it offers us a clearer insight as to the nature of sin, of redemption, and of our relationship with the God who shaped us all for a wondrous and beautiful purpose.

Chapter 3

A HISTORY OF FORGERY AND DECEPTION

They exchanged the truth about God for a lie, and worshiped
and served created things rather than the Creator.
ROMANS 1:25

Han van Meegeren was a brilliant Dutch artist active near the dawn of the twentieth century. He possessed an incredible eye for detail, and he produced paintings of astounding realism. Unfortunately for him, realism was not a coveted medium at that time. The realities of life were difficult in the early 1900s, and the populace was generally looking for something more imaginative and inspirational: an uplifting moment of reprieve to contrast the war, pandemic, and economic depression that had been so prevalent in their world. As a result, Han's detailed realism was the *last thing* that interested them. Instead, the artistic world was happily celebrating the avant-garde movement, a more eclectic style of brushwork, and colorful interpretation.

While Han was openly praised for his technical proficiency, his work was undesirable to many; and as a result, there was little market for his paintings. Feeling slighted, Meegeren sought revenge against the artistic community. Out of sheer spite, he was driven by a nefarious desire to humiliate those who had rejected his work. In Johannes Vermeer, the famed Dutch master from the late Renaissance period, Meegeren discovered the perfect mode of reprisal.

Vermeer's paintings were highly coveted, yet little was known about his early life, and it was rumored that many unknown works might still exist, though currently unidentified. As a result, many collectors kept an eager lookout for a potential "lost Vermeer masterpiece." This granted Han his perfect opportunity. He studied the works of the old master, painstakingly collecting the right wooden panels, the identical canvas, and the precise mixture of paints. He even custom-made a brush, similar to the one Vermeer had used. Han spent years developing the techniques necessary to make the perfect forgery, including a method of falsifying the age of his artistic hoaxes so they would appear to be hundreds of years older than they actually were. Through careful investigation, he discovered exactly what the art appraisers were looking for in a Vermeer original, and he purposefully mimicked those markers of authenticity.

Finally, in 1937, Meegeren's forgery depicting *The Last Supper* fell into the hands of Abraham Bredius, an esteemed art collector and Renaissance enthusiast. The painting was deemed to be an authentic lost Vermeer, and the art world erupted with excitement.

This allowed Meegeren to continue manufacturing a long string of counterfeits: a fraudulent portfolio that would ultimately culminate in a market value of over $30 million. His revenge was complete! He had fooled the art world and successfully lined his own pockets.

The success of Meegeren's deception wasn't simply based on his ability to mimic Vermeer's style and brushstroke; his true ability lay in preying on the desires of a community who *wanted* to believe his forgeries were authentic. He duped real people into investing real resources toward the acquisition of something that was fake, and it all began with an artist's wounded ego.

Han wasn't the first deceiver to successfully trick others into exchanging something real for something fraudulent. This clever deception can be traced back through time—even to the Garden of Eden. It was there that everything fell apart.

TROUBLE IN PARADISE

Consider the very beginning: the Garden of Eden, as described in the book of Genesis. The Garden is enshrined in human consciousness as a place of peace and tranquility, the very model of perfection.

- Adam and Eve existed in a perfect state of security. (There was no death, disease, discord, or danger.)
- They knew the beauty of identity. (They were loved, cherished, and created in the image of God Himself. The stamp of identity was clearly in, on, and around them.)
- They experienced independence. (God was not micromanaging them. In Genesis 2:19, we see God brought the creatures of the earth to Adam in order that he might name them, and whatever name Adam gave the animal, that's what it was. The world was theirs to explore and subdue.)
- They walked in significance. (As the crown jewel of creation, they were granted dominion over all the earth, with exclusive access to the Creator of the universe.)
- They knew innocence. (They had not yet been tainted by sin.)

Then enters the serpent. He's dejected and bitter—possibly even looking for revenge. It's worth noting that Satan did not offer Adam and Eve anything they didn't already possess. Yet ever the deceiver, the manipulator, the forgery artist, and the snake oil salesman, Satan pulled a slick move we now know to be the oldest trick in the book. That is to say, he convinced Adam and Eve to *switch* FCH providers. Rather than looking to God as the source of life and fulfillment, he persuaded them to search elsewhere, thus orchestrating the largest and most devastating con in human history. He turned Adam and Eve away from the real thing and toward the cheap counterfeit. This is the original sin, and its cataclysmic boom still echoes throughout creation.

The Devil began by calling into question their security and identity. He insinuated that God couldn't be trusted, that God really didn't care about them, and that God's primary interest was in keeping them down. Interestingly, the serpent's strategy hasn't changed one iota. Even today, he whispers the same dubious lie in our ears. Perhaps even now he is tempting you to look for help and solution outside of God's will, God's timing, and God's good design. Sowing discord, doubt, and suspicion is a long-used battle tactic, and it has proven more than effective for the serpent throughout the ages—even against God's own people.

Once the Devil had successfully undermined their *security* and *identity*, they were sufficiently weakened so as to be susceptible to his offer of counterfeit *independence* and *significance*. Satan insisted that disobeying God would lead to greatness, to a life-altering increase of wisdom and freedom. He said to them, "You will be like God" (Genesis 3:5). To the devastation of all, Adam and Eve took the bait, falling to his grand deception.

Besides being a liar and a manipulator, the Devil is perpetually delusional, so it is within the realm of possibility that he, at some level, actually believed what he was saying. Still, we know the *opposite* of Satan's inferred *greatness* and *freedom* is what followed. Consequences ensued, resulting in turmoil and death. The serpent effectively led Adam and Eve "down the garden path," convincing them to exchange the Masterpiece for the counterfeit. By the time they realized what had happened, the damage had already been done: they were exposed and afraid.

Adam and Eve exchanged *real security* and *identity* for counterfeit *independence* and *significance*, and in so doing, they rejected God and lost their *innocence*. What had begun in perfect paradise all came crashing down. The human soul was sent reeling off course, and mankind has been casting about in desperation ever since.

EVASIVE MANEUVERS

The testimony in Genesis is so frustrating, yet before I place all the blame on Adam and Eve, I must confess that I, too, have nibbled the serpent's bait. The plight of humanity today cannot simply be hung around the necks of Adam and Eve; it bursts forth from the sinful hearts of every man and every woman.

Observe what happened next. Even though they were divided and fallen, Adam attempted to regain something precious to him—something *so* precious he was willing to incriminate his wife in the hopes of reclaiming it. Adam essentially told God, "It was all Eve's fault."

Actually, it was worse than that. Adam brazenly hinted that God was to blame as well. He said to God,

> *The woman* you put here *with me*—she gave me *the fruit from the tree, and I ate it* (Genesis 3:12, emphasis added).

Wow! What a fascinating statement.

After eating the apple (or whatever fruit it was), it seems apparent that Adam had been scheming in the bushes, reeling from the early effects of sin, and hastily scripting what he was going to say when God showed up. Can you hear the not-so-subtle insinuation lurking within Adam's choice of words? An experienced defense attorney could not have phrased it better! In response to the first feelings of shame and guilt, Adam was developing the very first victim mentality. He was unscrupulously claiming that *other people* were responsible for his plight—*they* were responsible for his actions. What was Adam hoping to accomplish by submitting such an egregious claim? He was desperately hoping to regain *a sense of innocence*!

This "post-apple" conduct is worthy of note, as it casts a revealing spotlight on both *historic* and *modern* human behaviors. I, unfortunately, can detect this same Edenistic tendency skulking within my own elusive practices. How many times have I chosen Adam's "blame game" over that of honest confession? And all in an unadmirable attempt to deviously reassign culpability! My wife, my kids, my coworkers, the teller behind the desk at the vehicle registration office, the other driver on the freeway aggressively honking their horn as I hastily merge across traffic without signaling . . . each of them have borne the brunt of my Adam-like allegations.

And then, of course, there's Eve's ground-breaking indictment of the serpent. In the case of the Devil, it's obvious he *is* guilty of perpetual misconduct but, like Eve, my allegations against him are often evasive and self-serving. Similar to her husband, Eve's attempt to deflect blame was executed with legendary precision, but with her own personal flare and flamboyance. She essentially claimed, "The Devil made me do it!"

This may be the first slogan to successfully trend worldwide and throughout time. Even today, both believers and unbelievers alike continue to recite variations of her pretentious chant. However, it should be noted that the Devil can't *make* us do or feel anything. He can lie to us; he can seduce us; he can make false promises and promote false narratives; he can distort the truth and bait clever traps, but he can't *force* us into believing his fallacies. God is faithful, and He always provides a way out for us! This was just as true then as it is now. And while the serpent *was* judged to be complicit in Adam and Eve's downfall, "blaming the snake," accusing God, and denouncing each other did *not* absolve Adam and Eve of their personal guilt. In fact, their dishonest evasions only solidified their fallen state. The same can be said for each one of us.

I have often wondered how different things would be if, in addition to the first sin, Adam and Eve had also been the first to model honest repentance. Sadly, we will never know. We must deal with reality as it presently is, and throughout the remainder of our time together, my intent is to do exactly that.

CREATION VS. CREATOR

SECURITY—IDENTITY—INDEPENDENCE— SIGNIFICANCE—INNOCENCE

This is what Adam and Eve had. This is what Adam and Eve lost. This is what Adam and Eve tried to regain through fraudulent means. This is what your soul has always been craving!

From the Garden of Eden to this very day, the sin is not found in the craving. In fact, these soul cravings are God's design, and they exist for the good purpose of motivating us toward nourishment and fulfillment—of drawing us back to the home of His great heart! Effectively, these five cravings represent an exciting journey, one that God joyfully encourages each of us to embark upon. Craving security is a *good thing!* The pursuit of identity is a *noble* and *natural* pursuit! Our desire for innocence is both *beautiful* and *restorative.* What ultimately transforms these God-given cravings into sin is when we redirect them away from God (their true source of fulfillment) and toward lesser and fallen nouns, toward creations rather than the Creator. These "nouns" or "creations" are not always problematic in and of themselves, but when they are positioned *in the place of God,* they become the very sources of our distress.

For example, a mandarin orange is a tasty and nutritious treat. But if I repurpose the orange and begin using it as the hammer with which I expect to build my home, I will be disappointed. In this instance, the fault is not with the orange but with my distorted expectation of it. The same is true regarding your soul. Earthly resources cannot be expected to satisfy its cravings. Why? For the same reason we can't pump water into a gas tank and expect the engine to run properly or why we can't shampoo our hair with motor oil and expect it to be clean: it just wasn't designed to work that way. We are the same! Our natural (and original) relationship with God is a closely connected creation/Creator relationship! Meaning that, at the very core of our being, we are *custom designed* to walk with God, and no other existence can satisfy our souls. Adam and Eve discovered this pivotal truth about themselves mere moments after their debacle in the Garden, and we are blessed to have it proven to us on almost a daily basis.

One benefit of modern technology and media is that we now have a lens through which we can peer into the lives of the world's richest and most famous people. Truly, they have access to the most convincing counterfeits available. As we watch, we witness absurd, almost unimaginable wealth, lavish comfort, far-reaching influence, award-winning accomplishment, and the mingling of beautiful and eclectic personalities. What we do *not* witness is happiness, fulfillment, or peace, even though they are undoubtedly attempting to show us their "good side." Why? I again repeat—we are custom designed to walk with God, and no other existence will satisfy the human soul! Acts 17:28 clearly testifies to this, saying,

> *In him (our Maker) we live and move and have our being.*

Adam and Eve experienced the provision for all things in God Himself. Then they chose to believe a lie, and they exchanged God—*for an apple.* Consider the magnitude of that! Consider also that this tragic, self-annihilating exchange is one which the human race has continued to broker throughout the ages, including myself! I, sadly, have believed my fair share of lies. No doubt you also know what it means to be tangled in falsehood and pointed in the wrong direction. What heavenly joy and peace have we forfeited? And all because we've pursued happiness using a map drawn by a deceiving serpent!

The Holy Spirit, through the apostle Paul, dropped a truth bomb on the Church in Rome, stating of sinful man,

> *They exchanged the truth about God for a lie, and worshiped and served created things rather than the Creator* (Romans 1:25).

SECURITY—IDENTITY—INDEPENDENCE—
SIGNIFICANCE—INNOCENCE

Perhaps you have never identified them by name before, but as much as an unedited family portrait or selfie, these five cravings embody the raw and passionate pursuit of the human race. They are a picture of our hope and our desperation, simultaneously. We lost them in the Garden, and we've been scouring the globe in desperation ever since.

The purpose of these cravings is to draw us back to God, and yet, as Paul pointed out, mankind has distorted these cravings, assigning them as idols to be worshiped or fantasies to be conjured up.

Throughout the next few chapters, we will dissect and evaluate each of these cravings individually. We will expose distortions, identify variants, and marvel at God's boundless provisions of grace, mercy, and solution amid it all. Discovery awaits!

Chapter 4

IS IT SAFE?
(A CRAVING FOR SECURITY)

Big Tony could best be described as a chiseled piece of granite. He was huge, hard, and unfeeling. Furthermore, as an undiagnosed cancer ravaged his hulking body, his skin had increasingly become ashen—even gray in appearance. Big Tony was only thirty-one years old, but a life of hard living had aged him dramatically.

He wore a pinstripe suit stretched over his massive frame, and a well-kept fedora hat tipped slightly to the right. His normally dull and emotionless eyes were now flooded with concern as he watched his boss pace back-and-forth in clear distress. In all his years of working for Mr. Gabriel, he had never witnessed him behaving in such a tense and vulnerable manner. He found it unsettling.

Big Tony had grown up a street orphan on the darker side of Chicago, and he began working for Mr. Gabriel when he was just eleven years old. His first job was to linger outside the old brick warehouse on the corner of Skylark and Fairchild and inform Mr.

Carter (Mr. Gabriel's now deceased assistant) of any unusual activity in the area. Tony would spend long hours lurking in the shadow of the building, his young eyes and ears probing the community for inconsistencies. Every once in a while, a few of his fellow "street rats" would join him in playing a game of hopscotch or marbles on the sidewalk, but he never failed to keep a sharp lookout.

Back then, they called him *Little* Tony and, like most kids who'd been abused and mistreated, he had developed a keen eye for identifying any approaching drama or danger. It was almost a sixth sense. If Little Tony felt anything was out of the ordinary, his instructions were to bounce his ball against the warehouse door three times. Mr. Carter would then take care of the rest.

In exchange for his vigilance, he was permitted to sleep in the janitor's closet at The Gentlemen's Club (one of many establishments owned and operated by Mr. Gabriel). Tony was also granted access to scraps from the club kitchen. It was the most stable life he had ever known.

At age thirteen, he was promoted to an errand runner. At seventeen, towering high above his peers and with shoulders as wide as two men, he was henceforth referred to as *Big* Tony and promoted to "other things." Once a small, stoic, and nervous child, Tony had grown into a giant, cold, and merciless man, with a reputation that made people tremble. After Mr. Carter's unfortunate demise, Big Tony was elevated to serve as Mr. Gabriel's new right-hand man.

Mr. Gabriel became a father figure to Tony; some might even say a master—or a god (though they wouldn't dare say it out loud). Tony would never forget how Mr. Gabriel had rescued him from the streets, giving him both a home and a sense of purpose. Even now, twenty years later, there was nothing he wouldn't do for his boss. He was loyal to a fault, a fact that Mr. Gabriel had often taken full advantage of.

On this day, Big Tony felt the icy grip of apprehension as he watched his mentor manically stride the room. Something was wrong—*very* wrong. He knew better than to ask questions, but if something had gone sideways, he wanted to fix it. Finally, he asked, "What is it, boss? What's happened?"

Mr. Gabriel whirled around in a flash, his half-smoked cigar flinging hot ash across the room at the force of his turn. "She's gone!" he snapped. "That's what's wrong!"

"Who's gone?"

"Margaret's gone!" Mr. Gabriel roared, adding emphases to his shout with a dramatic swing of his arm.

Mr. Gabriel returned to pacing the floor while Big Tony stood silent, processing the information in his slow, methodical way.

Margaret was just a few years younger than Tony, and Mr. Gabriel had likewise taken her under his wing ... though for very different reasons. Margaret was widely considered to be "Mr. Gabriel's woman,"—a title thrust upon her without her consent. If she had run off, there was only one place he imagined she would go. The few people who were not completely terrified of Big Tony discovered him to be a good, albeit unresponsive listener, and Margaret would often confide in him.

He considered the situation a few moments longer, then grunted, "I'll find her, boss." Big Tony pivoted on his heel and left the room. For a man of his immense stature, he could move with surprising grace and speed when motivated.

Alone in his office, Mr. Gabriel locked the door (as was standard procedure when Big Tony wasn't by his side). He returned to his massive oak desk and sat down on a plush leather chair. Resting his forehead in his now trembling hands, he drew a long breath and exhaled slowly. *How could she leave me?* he thought bitterly—mournfully. He had promised himself he would never care for anyone this deeply ever again—but he had broken that promise for her. He cursed himself for behaving like a sentimental fool. Sure, he could be rough with her at times, but didn't she know he would kill for her? Big Tony would find her. He *had* to!

His private moment of rumination was interrupted by a sharp, rhythmic knock on the door. "Who is it?" he shouted irritably.

"It's me, boss." The smooth voice belonged to Skinny Pete.

Mr. Gabriel stood up, turning first to the beveled mirror that hung next to a portrait of his deceased wife. He quickly addressed any lingering signs of grief. If anyone other than Big Tony were ever to see him in this distressed condition he would quickly lose control of his entire crew. His men respected strength, cash, and nothing else. Satisfied with what he now saw reflecting back at him, he clenched his jaw and unlocked the door.

Having just watched Big Tony leave the building, Skinny Pete stood waiting—a 9 mm Luger clutched in his hand.

CRAVING SECURITY

As you consider the above story, I would invite you to take note of the differing securities our characters sought to possess and employ: locked doors, hulking associates, confident (yet manufactured) personas, profitable businesses, relational connections, shelter, strength, stealth, surveillance, physical senses, consistent meals, and secret hideaways. A ravenous desire for security motivated each of our characters into all manner of behaviors and life choices. And while their story may sound dated or fanciful to some, the cravings prompting each of them are no different from our own. I could've just as easily told the story of a suburban housewife or a cattle rancher, and the desire for security would've been just as evident.

Truthfully, we are *all* craving security. Mothers and fathers, politicians and nurses, soldiers and toddlers. Even the most heinous of criminals—the thug, the abuser, the murderer—will each go home and lock their doors at night to protect themselves from the same violation they just inflicted on someone else. The notorious Al Capone employed round-the-clock personal bodyguards. The brutal Mexican drug lord, El Chapo, spied on his own wife and lived in a bulletproof fortress equipped with underground escape routes. This desire for security is inherent within each of us.

America's first ambassador to the United Nations, Mr. E. R Stettinius, once allegorized the growth of a tree, saying,

> *There are many roots to happiness,*
> *but none more important than security.*

Security is a core human craving, and we will experience neither happiness nor peace without it. For certain, each precious moment enjoyed in the sunshine is reliant on the perception that we are physically and emotionally safe. Without this assurance, we are tense, exhaustively alert, and predictably unhappy. Without question, our desire for security permeates every aspect of our being, and any chance we have to experiencing abundant life will require that we address it.

As we seek to better understand this core craving, we can begin by dividing it into two primary categories: *physical security* and *relational security*. Ultimately, our desire for other securities (such as financial security or emotional security) all stem from our desire for physical and relational stability.

PHYSICAL SECURITY

The human craving for physical security is self-evident and well documented. In the field of psychology, it is often referred to as *the drive for self-preservation.* This is a very apt description, as this preservative instinct motivates us beyond mere *reactive* survival and into the proactive work of securing our securities. To this end, we employ our human ingenuity in a synchronized effort to neutralize the very real threats posed by the natural world: the threat of starvation or of dehydration, the threat of illness or the elements, of attack or uncertainty. We answer these potential threats by strengthening our supply chains, advancing our medical knowledge, and stockpiling weapons (even in times of peace) as a deterrent against currently unidentified enemies. We lock our doors, double-lock our safes, and establish societal laws, all in an effort to achieve, preserve, and enhance our sense of physical security.

Mr. Gabriel sought security in hired muscle, padlocks, a thick wallet, and personal persona. Big Tony and Margaret were first driven to Mr. Gabriel while searching for the security of a warm bed and a warm meal. Indeed, many people have willingly suspended their moral values in exchange for little more than food and shelter. As a result, some now believe our *will to live* is the greatest of all human drives, but I would suggest this hypothesis to be wanting. Our craving for security is not that simple. Physical security *is* indeed a fundamental desire, and yet, our everyday lives resound with examples of individuals willing to risk their physical safety in an attempt to impress or connect with someone else. Sometimes we call them daredevils, thrill seekers, or even just "lovestruck fools," but their motivations are actually very commonplace. Indeed, we only label them with such titles when we are fortunate enough to be detached from their very real sense of urgency or desperation.

Without question, our craving for relational security is *so tenacious,* it can drive each of us to willingly risk (or even sacrifice) our physical security to gain, maintain, or enhance the relational aspect.

(Side note: The aforementioned "daredevils" and "thrill seekers" might also risk their physical security in the pursuit of identity, independence, significance, or innocence.)

RELATIONAL SECURITY

Perhaps our craving for relational security can best be described as the insatiable desire to care for someone and to have someone care for us. Reciprocal affection! Love! We long for the security of knowing that our hearts are safe in the hands of those who hold them, and we can literally be driven to a point of madness if this security fails.

This craving for love, acceptance, and affirmation is at the very core of our favorite stories. It is a unifying thread between all genres and generations. England will recite the ballad of Romeo and Juliet, China of Liang Shanbo and Zhu Yingtai, India of Mirza and Sahiba, all tragic love stories highlighting the prominence that every culture places on the relational security we are craving in human connection. This coveted connection is not merely found in romance but in family and friendship as well. Sadly, the connections we attempt to establish are not always helpful or healthy. Big Tony sought a father-son connection with Mr. Gabriel—who shamelessly exploited it. Mr. Gabriel tried to *force* a connection on Margaret—who understandably didn't reciprocate. Indeed, it is not uncommon for us to do desperate things in our pursuit of secure relational connection.

In the absence of a sufficient human relationship, some individuals may attempt to compensate through connection with a pet or, in extreme cases, an imaginary friend. It has even been suggested that future humanity will increasingly turn to interactive technologies to have their relational cravings satisfied. We can debate whether we believe these compensations to be healthy or helpful. Nonetheless, it is abundantly clear that we can gain access to all the money, power, fame, and sex in the world, but if our lives are devoid of relational security, we will find neither happiness nor peace.

SECURITY INSIGHTS

This hunger for security is what drives our incessant want of insurance, guarantee, contract, promise, and vow. In negative practice, it can tempt us toward demanding control issues. You show me someone who is obsessed with control, and I'll show you someone who is desperately seeking security—or significance.

My wife and I were confronted with these same issues early in our marriage. We had both experienced the pain of rejection and volatility in our youth and were each determined never to experience it again. Unfortunately, our method of determination was all wrong, resulting in repeated attempts to bully and dominate each other. At times (in an effort to prop up my insecurities), I would place self-serving and suffocating controls upon her, thus violating her craving for reasonable independence. At other times, she would use the power of her tongue to shame and accuse me, cutting me down verbally and squashing my combined craving for identity and innocence (i.e., my need to believe that I was worth something). Little did we know, we were each triggering the other at the most sensitive point of our wound, and all this in an unconscious effort to gain control over the very person we claimed to love. Needless to say, our relationship was extremely volatile. It was the exact *opposite* of the relational security we were hoping to experience in our marriage.

Thankfully, with the help of godly counselors and by God's grace, we have gradually been able to heal and mature. Interestingly, when finally pointed in the right direction, it became apparent that God had divinely intended my wife to play an important role in *my* healing and I in hers. We realized that we were *not* incompatible opposites; rather, we were united in a common craving and called to submit hand-in-hand before our Heavenly Physician.

Once we understood this truth about ourselves and each other, healthy communication and connection became much easier, and our sense of relational security increased dramatically. I consider us fortunate, as many unhappy people live year after year without ever gaining the beauty and power of self-awareness. My prayer is that this book will help trigger a fresh awakening for many.

It should also be mentioned that self-awareness is not an indefinite state of being—and neither is relational connection. Any awakening (or connection) we experience must be purposefully maintained through humility, honesty, and grace. Courage is also necessary, as the most intimidating person you will ever confront about these issues will be yourself. And when faced with ourselves, we are often discovered to exhibit pious, evasive, judgmental, and boorish tendencies (hence the required humility, honesty, grace, and courage).

WHERE CAN I FIND IT?

We are *all* craving physical and relational security, but in a world of decay, aggression, betrayal, and confusion, where can it be found? Just when we think we've discovered it, it proves itself fragile. People will move into your life and then away. Economies will grow and then diminish. Earthly governments will rise and fall. The pattern is clear: wood rots, steel rusts, ships sink, guns jam, technology malfunctions, hearts break, pets and people pass away—even our little blue planet is likely to fail at some point. So where can we find security? Perhaps we haven't officially asked the question, but at this very moment, billions of souls are desperately scouring the globe (and even the stars) in search of the answer.

Satan suggested to Adam and Eve that satisfaction for our craving could be realized in the expansion of personal wisdom, position, and power. However, this "garden variety" solution contains a fatal flaw: it's man-centric, thus making it inherently fallible. Unfortunately, faith in the fallible has been our oft-repeated folly since Genesis.

In Psalm 20:7, King David sings,

> *Some trust in chariots and some in horses,*
> *but we trust in the name of the LORD our God.*

As I consider his words, I note that both the religious and the irreligious alike are searching for security—and *both* are placing their faith in a specific source to deliver it. One looks toward chariots and horses (i.e., earthly resources and solutions), the other toward God. Contrary to the opinion of some, faith is not isolated to the lives of those traditionally referred to as "the religious." Every day, the general public will board airplanes without ever catching sight of the pilot or the maintenance crew. Such an action requires faith. We daily eat foods without ever really knowing where the food came from or with what chemicals they have been sprayed. Again, that's faith.

Think even of the theory of evolution. It is clearly labeled a "theory," and yet many hundreds of millions have placed their faith in its murky explanation for our very existence. Such existential trust requires as much faith (if not more) than the most religious of religions.

My point is this: faith is as universally exercised as breathing, but our security is only as stable as the noun upon which our faith is placed. Knowing this, King David made his allegiance clearly known; while certain others were trusting in various creations, David was trusting in the Creator.

This begs me to ask a few important questions of myself, "Which camp am I truly in? In what sources have I placed my security?" I like to think I am strongly positioned in the *Lord our God* camp, that I have chosen a God-based security system over that of chariots and horses—but have I really? All too often, the testimony evidenced by my behavior shouts in stark contrast to the rose-colored affidavit sworn by my imagination. In other words, I am not always who I like to think I am!

> MY POINT IS THIS: FAITH IS AS UNIVERSALLY EXERCISED AS BREATHING, BUT OUR SECURITY IS ONLY AS STABLE AS THE NOUN UPON WHICH OUR FAITH IS PLACED.

Sadly, it is not uncommon for a Christian to hear the Word of God, to have their hearts leap in excitement at its truth, only to have their will (that center which produces action) lag sluggishly behind. The bill passes unanimously in the legislature of the mind, only to stall in the senate of implementation. Indeed, it is possible for us to naïvely *imagine* a deeper faith than we actually practice.

The apostle Peter serves as a classic example of this nasty discrepancy. When it came to all things Jesus, Peter was always at the front of the line, demanding to be both seen and heard. Nobody could question his enthusiasm and affection for Jesus. Peter insisted he would never abandon his Rabbi, that he would follow Him every step of the way, and that Christ was everything to him. It was even Peter who said to Jesus, "You have the words of eternal life" (John 6:68), and then the rooster crowed, and Peter's divided heart was laid bare. With a flood of despair, Peter realized he wasn't the "believer" he thought he was. It was a rude and devastating awakening, and yet such an awakening may be necessary for each of us should we refuse to be woken up in a gentler fashion.

In truth, many Christians spend year after year exercising the pre-rooster faith of Peter. They languish in double-mindedness and conflicting securities, saying "amen" to truths they are not yet willing to live. Oh, that we would experience a bounty of metaphorical roosters in our own lives, holy cockerel sent to awaken us to ourselves. Peter's moment of agonizing self-discovery helped calibrate his will to his heart, and eventually, it grew him into a true spiritual giant. The same heavenly growth is possible for each one of us, but it begins with honesty. And so I again ask the question, "Where do I find my security? Truly?"

HEAVENLY PROVISION

In the book of Psalms, we witness our core humanities on full display, and each chapter reads like a raw essay on the human condition. This honest diary of a sinful soul offers hope for the entire world as even amid desperate turmoil, God is revealed to be a Strong Tower, a constant help in times of trouble. He is the Deliverer, an unfailing Father who would care for us even when our earthly parents forsake us.

Among the many assurances declared in the scriptures, four echo repeatedly throughout David's symphony:

- God's love will endure forever.
- God's justice will always prevail in the end.
- God Himself will watch over you with love and strength.
- God's Word will never fail.

This is our stability! This is where true security rests, in none other than the good promises of God Himself! We are all craving security, and this is the answer!

Chances are, *you already knew this answer*. You learned it years ago in Sunday school or youth group—yet the problem has remained stubbornly unresolved. Throughout the remaining chapters, we will identify several practical steps you can take toward finally *implementing* the answer and therein finding true rest for the soul.

With a heart of full transparency, Jesus warns us of the trouble we will face in this fallen world: rejection, loss, betrayal, persecution, and failure. He then offsets these discouraging realities with the joy of every believer, saying, "Take heart! I have overcome the world" (John 16:33).

In Christ Jesus, every despair can be washed away by hope, every failure by redemption, every sin by forgiveness, and all death by life. God has offered each of us the opportunity to cast our anxieties upon Him—*all* of them! God's love, power, grace, and faithfulness contain the provision for our *every* security need. Deep within us, our core humanity is diligently at work, gently, yet persistently, guiding us toward this place of happy rest. Like iron, we are being drawn to the magnetic heart of God. His heart is faithful and strong and fully deserving of our trust.

Dear Heavenly Father,

I ask that you open the eyes of my heart. Grant me the vision to see the abundance of security that is found only in You. Forgive me for believing the serpent's lie, for pursuing the counterfeit, for my foolish pride. Lord, I believe in Your power and goodness, and I ask You to help me overcome any remaining and debilitating unbelief. I invite you to do a great work in my heart and in my mind. Please grant me the strength and discernment necessary to successfully reposition the direction of my hope. Thank You for never abandoning me. I want to trust You more! Help me to elevate my thinking, my vision, my faith. Amen.

SECURITY REFLECTION JOURNAL

- What area of security causes you the most anxiety? (Circle any that apply to your circumstance.)

(1) Physical | (2) Relational | (3) Financial | (4) Other (explain) | (5) All

- What truths does God want you to know about Himself in order to ease the tension within you?
  1. _____
  2. _____
  3. _____

- What practical and tangible steps can you take in surrendering these anxieties to God?
  1. _____
  2. _____
  3. _____

- Without self-righteously judging someone else, is there anyone you can think of who may struggle with this specific craving? How can you use this fresh awareness to better understand and love them?

NOTES:

_____
_____
_____
_____
_____
_____
_____
_____
_____
_____
_____
_____
_____
_____
_____
_____
_____
_____

Chapter 5

WHO AM I?
(A CRAVING FOR IDENTITY)

When John and Jane stepped into my office for premarital counseling, it quickly became apparent that they needed to sort through some serious identity issues.

Much has been made regarding codependency in recent years—so much so, the definition of the term has become somewhat varied. In the context of this chapter, a codependent person is an individual who struggles to find any identity apart from their primary relationship. In other words, their whole sense of being is completely dependent upon their connection with someone else. In essence, the codependent mantra says, "If there is no we, there is no me." An immature person might consider such a mantra to be romantic, but in reality, it can be devastating. When a relationship ends or becomes volatile, it is natural for a healthy person to experience heartbreak. But a codependent person will experience heartbreak, *amplified considerably* by the addition of a full-fledged identity crisis. They didn't just lose their partner, they also lost themselves.

In rare cases, a codependent relationship *might* work, provided all parties (without coercion) mutually agree to practice this dangerous level of identity dependency. That said, it is generally unsustainable. Trouble looms large on the horizon when only one member desires to remain codependent, and things can become messy (and even abusive) when one partner *insists* the other be codependent upon them. This was the case with John and Jane.

While Jane communicated her dream to be a mother and a part-time realtor, John aggressively shut down the conversation, bluntly declaring, "I just want you to be my wife—and nothing else." Throughout several sessions of counseling, it became apparent that he literally saw her as *one thing*, and he wanted her to identify herself the same way. This dominating and oppressive pattern kept revealing itself in our sessions together, and I recognized it for what it was, having struggled with it myself as a young man. I then encouraged them to receive some one-on-one counseling prior to making their vows.

For one human to insist that another rest their identity *entirely* upon them is neither reasonable nor healthy. It certainly isn't love. It reeks more of egocentric obsession, likely stemming from a childhood wound. Such a marriage would soon become a battleground of manipulation, power struggle, and resentment. This makes codependency an unstable union.

Interdependency, however, is very healthy in a marriage. It happens when two people (with firmly established personal identities) make the purposeful commitment to entwine those identities together. Independently, they possess strength, but together they are stronger. Side by side, they can help each other grow, flourish, and even heal. This beautiful merging of hearts begins the powerful collaboration of souls we call *a family*. Such a union does not end personal identity; rather, it strengthens, affirms, and even expands it.

WHAT IS IDENTITY?

Identity: academically defined as *psychological identification* (IDEM).

The quest for identity is a quest that all of humanity will embark upon. Ultimately, we are seeking to answer four symbiotic questions:

- Who am I?
- What is my purpose?
- Where do I belong?
- Do I have value?

From an early age, your soul will ask these questions of you, and your answers must be *personalized* first and then shared second. The shared aspect of identity is vitally important; still, leapfrogging over the personal and delving straight into the shared generally leads to codependency and unhappy volatility.

As mentioned in the previous chapter, you may possess an abundance of wealth, power, fame, and health; but if you can't answer the questions of identity with confidence, you will not experience lasting peace—period! This is why history is chock-full of individuals who "had it all" but were secretly sad and depressed, addicted to substances, and living in desperation—even to the point of deciding that life wasn't worth living.

This search for identity is the search for personal identification. First, we seek to answer the questions, "Who am I, and what is my purpose?" Then we look for the support of affiliation and validation by asking, "Where do I belong, and do I have value?" In a sense, we are seeking a label, not unlike the label in the grocery store that says "Peaches" and then points down to a box that is full of juicy, delicious peaches. To be clear, we are not seeking *any* label. We seek a label that identifies us as something of value and purpose, a banner that proudly declares, "This is who I am! This is where I belong!"

Our craving for identity is why the old adage "Sticks and stones may break my bones, but words can never hurt me" is verifiably untrue. Sticks and stones may break my bones, but cruel names and labels (if I choose to believe them) *can wound my soul,* the very core of who I am, by destabilizing my sense of identity. We are very susceptible to this type of harm during our formative years, but truthfully, many remain vulnerable throughout the entirety of their earthly lives.

IDENTITY LOST

Without the tether of a healthy and secure identity, happiness and peace will quickly drift beyond our grasp. One of our first and most impactful introductions to identity is found in relation to our caregivers. Every child longs to know they are cherished! We need to grow up confidently sensing that we are both *wanted* and *valued!* This is the first place we seek to experience psychological identification, a sense of personal value, and shared belonging. But if we *don't* discern it within our family unit (or if we are coerced and confused by various identity propagandas), it can trigger a chain reaction, one often leading to heartache and confusion, a sad and desperate quest that employs sad and desperate strategies. Subconsciously, we begin scheming,

Maybe if I have sex with this person, they will think I am worth something. Maybe if I do drugs, I will discover myself (or the pain will end). Maybe if I steal something, this group will accept and affirm me. Maybe I should experiment with this or that; maybe then I'll be wanted, maybe then someone will claim me, maybe then I'll find the place where I belong.

Another possibility is that I simply withdraw into myself (or into fantasy), where I erect high walls to protect my heart from the hurt of not knowing who I am or where I belong. Many parents are rightly concerned that their children are hiding from life in their video games, yet they remain blind to the fact that they themselves are modeling a similar evasion through social media or other online obsessions.

An identity crisis is a big deal. It is a primary cause of depression and despair, potentially resulting in self-mutilation or even suicide. If I do not know my identity, I will spend my life in desperate (and sometimes damaging) experimentation as I search for psychological identification, validation, and affiliation. A broken relationship, broken trust, job loss, abuse, and personal trauma can all lead to an identity crisis, identity lost.

IDENTITY FOUND

Knowing your identity is beautiful. Perhaps the best way to describe the euphoria of knowing your identity would be to say, *identity feels like home!* It's that place where you *know* you belong: warm, comfortable, stable, and safe. It's precious to you, which is why you will fight to defend it.

Even in the search for love, we can observe the human quest for identity. In someone's claim to love me, I feel valuable. I feel wanted. I feel a sense of belonging, and to that end, in searching for identity, we don't merely seek to find; we also crave *to be found*. We yearn to hear someone say the words, "I choose you. We belong together."

Whether they are healthy or unhealthy, the identities we adopt are not easily replaced or exchanged. We hold a tight grip on them, and they hold a tight grip on us. This can be very comforting, stabilizing, and wonderful; however, it can also add longevity to trauma or be used to manipulate us as for better or for worse, our identity will be the most powerful factor when determining our allegiances.

IDENTITY MANIPULATION

Have you noticed how modern advertisements are less promoting a product or experience and are more attempting to sell you an identity? Why is that? It's simple logic: if you adopt their product, their experience, their ideology (or their candidate) *as your identity*, they can count on you to support and prosper them for many years to come—whether their product remains a quality product or not.

Once you adopt something as an identity, you will keep purchasing, keep subscribing, keep voting, and keep believing everything that is offered or promoted to you. It creates the ultimate long-lasting loyalty, even when loyalty ceases to be wise, safe, or legal. There is ample evidence to demonstrate that your sense of identity will shape (and possibly even override) your moral code of right and wrong, truth and justice, and even your health and safety. That is to say, identity can cause moral, ethical, and logical blindness.

How and why? When you feel you've found your IDEM (i.e., your *shared* identity), it is precious to you, and you will cling desperately to it. This is why most people won't tell the police about a family member who has committed a crime. It's why a battered wife finds it so hard to leave her spouse even though he repeatedly punches her black and blue. It's why it takes far too long for someone in a college fraternity to blow the whistle on a hazing ritual that has gone way too far. It's also why politics has grown so hostile and political discussion so unsafe, as we sadly have become less interested in the healthy exchange of differing ideas and more interested in the aggressive expansion of our political identity. More than ever, people are less likely to vote regarding "the issues" and more likely to vote in relation to partisan association.

IT'S WHY A BATTERED WIFE FINDS IT SO HARD TO LEAVE HER SPOUSE EVEN THOUGH HE REPEATEDLY PUNCHES HER BLACK AND BLUE.

Our identities can even affect how we dispense justice. For example, if someone is accused of committing a crime, they have the right to stand before a jury of their peers—so long as they aren't *too* peer-like. Prosecuting attorneys will go to great lengths to ensure the jury isn't filled with individuals who share the defendant's IDEM, for shared identity tends to make us biased and then farewell to truth and justice—goodbye to making a fair judgment based on real evidence. The reverse is also true. Justice is less assured when the jury box is filled with individuals who are *hostile* to the defendant's IDEM.

Truly, our human quest for identity impacts everything around us and within us. Sadly, this noble pursuit has been complicated in recent years by the continued breakdown of the family unit and a shrinking sense of both patriotism and religion—even through a heightened confusion regarding sex and sexuality. All this inner and social turmoil has resulted in an unprecedented identity crisis, and this growing uncertainty is *actively* being preyed upon by murky individuals, propagandists, and even corporations, each seeking to gain personal profit, pleasure, and advantage.

For the sake of our physical, mental, and spiritual well-being, it is crucial that we each develop a strong *primary identity*. An established primary identity stabilizes the soul in the midst of life's storms, and it faithfully reminds you *who you are*. Secondary, or peripheral identities can also be enjoyed (e.g.., hard-core sports fan, sales manager, outdoor enthusiast, armchair political pundit, etc.), so long as they remain fully aligned with your *primary*. If your identities conflict or compete with each other, the result will be instability and confusion. Unfortunately, this brand of inner conflict is not uncommon.

IDENTITY CONFUSION

The Israelites who were led out of Egypt are a prime example of unhealthy identity confusion. They had left Egypt, but Egypt had not yet left *them*. Whether they felt a certain sense of prestige at the role they played in the greatness that was Egypt or whether it was just the natural result of spending a long time in one place, either way, Egypt had imprinted itself on their consciousness. The land of the pharaohs had become an identity for them. It was not a total identity but a competing and contradictory influence, one with adverse effects that would ultimately prove devastating.

While God was leading His people safely through the Red Sea, the Egyptian treasure (which the Israelites carried in their luggage) was worming its way into their hearts. This resulted in identity confusion, a distortion that fully revealed itself in dramatic fashion through the creation of the golden calf. They made an Egyptian idol—*and they dared to put God's Name on it!* In other words, their distorted reasoning was so expansive that they struggled to differentiate between the true God of Israel and the pagan gods of Egypt.

I experience the same temptation regarding the Israelites of the Exodus as I do with Adam and Eve; I want to ridicule them for making such idiotic decisions. I want to roll my eyes and look down my nose at them. However, (and this is painful to admit), I realize that I may not be so different. I call myself a Christian (this, by definition, is my *primary identity*), but I am uncomfortably aware of *other* identities vying for lordship in my life. My discomfort grows as I realize that I am not a victim of these competing identities. They are here at *my* invitation! If I summon the courage to face myself further, I am confronted with the realization that I have built my own collection of golden calves, and on a portion of them, I have even dared to carve God's Name. At times, my distorted reasoning is similar to that of the Israelites of Egypt and, like them, I am oblivious to my contradictions.

Consuming relational attachments, career ambitions, and political allegiances—if we are not careful, these can become competing (and even hostile) identities, each seeking to dethrone Christ. Or at the very least, they arrogantly demand that the God of the universe shares His throne with them.

C. S. Lewis warns of this double-minded distortion in his brilliant book *The Screwtape Letters*, in which he issues caution regarding the dangers of becoming what he calls a "Christian and" (a person of faith claiming multiple and contradictory allegiances simultaneously).

IDENTITY COLLISIONS

I once heard the story of a man who was secretly married to three women at the same time. He even had children with two of the women. These wives *had no idea* their husband was living a triple life; they simply believed he was a businessman who traveled frequently at the behest of his company. Through major holidays, birthdays, even family vacations, unbelievably, this man was able to maintain his charade for several years. Eventually, predictably, it all came crashing down in a mess of heartache and confusion. Years later, the man admitted in an interview that he had never intended to create such a grand deception. Essentially, a conflicted heart led to the first web of lies, which led to another lie, and then another conflicted heart, and then more lies—a tangled web woven in confusion and desperation (with a fair amount of egomania sewn in).

AS EACH IDENTITY CREATES ITS OWN VALUE METRIC, OFFERS ITS OWN REWARD, AND DEMANDS ITS OWN ALLEGIANCE, CONFLICT BECOMES INESCAPABLE.

Whether our actions are based in naivety or arrogance, our adoption of multiple identities can be similarly distressing. As each identity creates its own value metric, offers its own reward, and demands its own allegiance, conflict becomes inescapable. Suddenly, to keep up the charade, internal lies will need to be told and moral contradictions self-justified. The individuals practicing this cryptic form of spiritual or moral polygamy can quickly find themselves trapped in a snare of hypocrisy and contradiction. Pressure mounts as they attempt to align themselves with contrary worldviews simultaneously. Eventually, it culminates in the sin of James 3, where both blessings and curses come flowing from the same mouth. Unfortunately, this harmful level of identity confusion is not uncommon.

The "Christian and" sabotages their opportunity to experience true peace and happiness by diluting their Christ identity with vain ambitions and worldly allegiances. In essence, they paint over the original with the counterfeit. Such individuals never experience lasting peace as they are perpetually rent in inner conflict—conflict that rages as contradictory identities battle for influence and dominion. Tozer also speaks to this issue, quipping, "In the 'and' lies our greatest woe."

Beware of the accumulation of contradictory identities; you are creating a war zone in which there can be no peace. Such a hostile collection will inevitably trap you in the perpetuity of unfulfilled desire, as quality is choked by unholy quantity. Sadly, this is a continuum in which many live and die, including Christians. It doesn't have to be this way. It *shouldn't* be this way. We must use caution regarding how we finish the sentence "I am a _____," for the phrase "I am" is an identity statement, and if it is not applied in accordance with God's good timing and design, it will ultimately lead to emptiness and turmoil.

HEAVENLY PROVISION

SO GOD CREATED MANKIND IN HIS OWN IMAGE.
—GENESIS 1:27

It always circles back to the *intimacy* and the *wonder* of this statement. You are *not* the result of galactic happenstance. You are *not* the random evolution of cells. You are purposefully and lovingly created in the image of your Heavenly Father. This reality is your *natural primary*! We are all craving identity, but only in returning to our Image Maker do we find that place where we can truly feel at home.

The story of the prodigal son (Luke 15) lends a beautiful allegory to this tragic leaving and joyous returning. The prodigal arrogantly left his rightful place and went out in pursuit of what the world had to offer. He tried on several new identities: party planner, sexual deviant, food production assistant, and a likely myriad of others left to the imagination. Truly he immersed himself in some of the world's most popular endeavors, but all he discovered was an empty and unsustainable existence. Finally, the blessed hour of self-revelation came (one which I pray would come to each of us). As with many revelations, it had to battle its way past pride and pretense, gaining its final victory through honest repentance. Such is the story of the prodigal. He finally returned home, and the celebration that greeted him upon his arrival was a sight to behold. This same celebration awaits each one of us upon our return from the wasteland of our wanderings. Together with our Heavenly Father at last, we find the place we truly belong.

At this point, someone might ask, "But doesn't the primary identity you are describing here essentially equate to a codependency upon God? And didn't you previously state that codependence is generally unhealthy?" The answer is *yes*; however, the volatility of codependency lies within the fallibility of our codependents. This is why codependence on God is the only model that actually works: He *alone* is unfailing! Furthermore, He alone is the Mold from which we are naturally cast!

The whole world is desperately craving identity. Unfortunately, we often pursue fulfillment in fallible places: notoriety, sexuality, worldly allegiance, and various vanities. Sooner or later, these counterfeits will be exposed for what they are.

God designed you with a great and loving purpose, and only in Christ can we find what we are looking for. Or to borrow a visual from a fairytale, "There is only one slipper that fits." I rather suppose the author of the fairytale discovered this literary inspiration within his own craving to belong.

Throughout the scriptures, you are granted valuable and meaningful identification: a child of God, the chosen of God, the image bearer of your Heavenly Father, the clear apple of His eye.

Perhaps the popular Christmas poem "Oh Holy Night" unwittingly describes it best.

> *Long lay the world in sin and error pining,*
> *till He appeared, and the soul felt its worth.*

Apart from God, our identity is uncertain, transient, feeble, and pining. Jesus enters this confusion and brings clarity, reminding us exactly who we are and where we belong.

Your entire life you have been searching for identity, for purpose, for meaning: you, me, and the whole world. Have you been looking in the right places? Just as the earthly father celebrated with the return of his prodigal son, in like manner, our Heavenly Father joyfully welcomes us back to the home of His everlasting arms.

Dear Heavenly Father,

I need to know who I am. I want to know this, not through mere head knowledge, but in the very depths of my soul. I ask Your forgiveness for the rooms in my heart that I have thoughtlessly rented out to competing and damaging identities. Make clear to me what repentance should look like in this context. Please cleanse me from my double-minded ways. Thank You for giving me purpose. Thank You for calling me YOURS, even as You are mine. Thank You for claiming me despite my many flaws and failures. Thank You for being the answer to my urgent questions.

Amen

IDENTITY REFLECTION JOURNAL

- What do you claim as your primary identity?

- Can you identify any competing identities currently occupying territory in your own life? (For your records, consider listing them below.)
  1. _____
  2. _____
  3. _____

- What steps need to be taken to cancel their lease on your identity?
  1. _____
  2. _____
  3. _____

- Without self-righteously judging someone else, is there anyone you can think of who may struggle with this specific craving? How can you use this fresh awareness to better understand and love them?

NOTES:

_____
_____
_____
_____
_____
_____
_____
_____
_____
_____
_____
_____
_____
_____
_____
_____
_____
_____
_____

Chapter 6

LET ME BE ME!
(A CRAVING FOR INDEPENDENCE)

The first thing you may think of when you hear the word *independence* is the Fourth of July or the words of William Wallace from the movie *Braveheart*:

You may take our lives, but you will never take our freedom.

What did William Wallace mean by freedom? What do any of us mean when we talk about freedom? Most commonly, we are referencing our right to self-determination, to individual thought and practice, and to choose our own destiny. Those who are "free" experience personal autonomy, but our craving for independence goes far beyond the desire for political, social, or even personal freedom. It is also the craving for distinct individuality: the desire to be set apart.

FREEDOM

Let me share a word of warning to every politician, every domineering spouse, parent, or person in a position of power or authority: *If you attempt to take away or restrict another individual's sense of freedom or individuality, sooner or later, you will be faced with a revolution.*

Yes, we may crave the security found in the collective or the identity found in shared partnership, but not at the expense of at least some sense of autonomy. It is part of being human. I would again assert that these cravings are not merely psychological. While the study of neuroscience and psychiatry can help explain our cognitive processes (i.e., how the biological mind functions), it is crucial we acknowledge that the mind itself is not the source of our cravings. Our core humanities are rooted much deeper, emanating from the *non*biological part of each one of us, the eternal soul. It was in response to this deeper call that Martin Luther King Jr. bravely climbed the steps of the Lincoln Memorial in 1963 and inspirationally quoted the lyric of Samuel Francis Smith, "From every mountainside let freedom ring."

Or who could forget the immortal words of Patrick Henry on the eve of the Revolutionary War in 1775. "Give me liberty, or give me death!"

These men didn't just speak for America; they spoke for every member of the human race. Freedom is not simply a societal preference; it is a moral demand, an unquenchable craving of the human soul. Even tyrants, those scoundrels who seek to take away the freedom of others, will themselves express personal outrage if they sense their own autonomy is being infringed upon.

We are all craving freedom.

INDIVIDUALITY

The cry for independence is not just a cry for freedom; it is a craving that burns deep within us for individuality, the desire to feel unique. We need to know there is something about us that sets us apart from everyone else. This is even true of those rare identical twins who seem to enjoy sporting the same haircuts and wearing the same clothing. Eventually, they will crave *something* that sets them apart as individuals. Maybe they're the athletic twin, the academic twin, or the social twin—they will search for *some* differential that sets them apart as distinct. We are all united in this desire.

If we do not possess a sense that we are unique, we will soon feel unseen, redundant, overlooked, unappreciated, lost, or unnecessary. If this becomes the case, no amount of security, identity, or autonomy will bring peace to our souls.

SAFE INDEPENDENCE

God answers our call for independence. In fact, He created it, and He placed the desire for it in our hearts—even as a reflection of Himself. God cannot be contained in a box, and neither can our cravings. Without freedom of movement and expression, without uniqueness of design and perspective, we would reflect a false image of God, for our reflection of Him would be one-dimensional and boring.

The book of Romans teaches that creation itself gives testimony to the power and even the nature of God. Just as we can learn something about a painter by inspecting his paintings, we glean information about God by considering His creations. This is particularly true of humanity, for we bear the likeness of our

Heavenly Father. Our sin obstructs the view, but if you can see your way around it, toward the core cravings God placed within each one of us, we can learn something about who *He* is. In the case of independence, we see a God who loves variety, a Father who delights in watching His children grow, mature, and blaze a unique path forward.

As God's children, we are His dependents. This dependency extends throughout every facet of existence—from the daily rising of the sun to the continued beating of our hearts. Still, don't mistake your dependence for a lack of independence. God has granted us the most perfect form of independence possible: *safe independence!* This is worthy of celebration, as not all forms of independence are safe; in fact, certain forms are downright dangerous. Throughout the scriptures, we observe God releasing and empowering His people to govern and steward, to imagine and create, to explore and expand, to enjoy bounty and even sex, all under the protection of His perfect Word.

God's Word plays an important role in the exercise of safe independence. Here's how it works: God grants us independence *in* Him and *with* Him—but not *from* Him. The latter is where our God-given craving becomes harmful, which is why God calls it sin. Why is independence *from* God a sin? Is it because God is an oppressive controller? Is He an overbearing Father? That is what the serpent would have you believe. That is what much of the world has become convinced of. The truth, however, is far different. God places boundaries on our behavior for the express purpose of protecting and elevating us. In other words, God's Word was sent to keep us from harm and help us succeed.

THE SIN NATURE

At this stage, I feel it's important to pause and introduce another key player actively engaged in our human story: the *sin nature*. Perhaps more than any other variable, this malicious force introduces stress and distortion into our personal, social, and spiritual lives. While its ramifications extend across the full spectrum of our human experience, there is no better time to spotlight its destructive influence then while discussing healthy boundaries and personal liberties.

In a purely secular/political letter sent to those who had participated in the French Revolution of 1789, Edmund Burke wrote these insightful words:

> *What is liberty if not accompanied by wisdom and virtue? It is the greatest of all possible evils!*

His point was this: freedom without barriers will inevitably result in our demise—in the greatest of all evils! Why? The answer is found in the self-destructive sin nature lurking within mankind. Both biblical and secular history unite to produce thousands of years of evidence for this fact.

In his book, *Notes from Underground*, a literary work that has been heralded by psychologists for 150-plus years, legendary author and philosopher Dostoevsky says of mankind,

> *Shower upon him every earthly blessing, drown him in a sea of happiness, so that nothing but bubbles of bliss can be seen on the surface; give him economic prosperity, such that he should have nothing else to do but sleep, eat cakes and busy himself with the con-*

tinuation of his species, and even then, out of sheer
ingratitude, sheer spite, man would play you some
nasty trick. He would even risk his cakes and would
deliberately desire the most fatal rubbish, the most
uneconomical absurdity, simply to introduce into all
this positive good sense, his fatal fantastic element.

While I do not propose Dostoevsky to be a biblical authority on anything, his writings, nonetheless, offer us an unfiltered and insightful glimpse into the chaotic heart of mankind. What he describes as the "fatal fantastic element" I liken to our systemic sin, which is by nature self-deprecating. To inject a small measure of humor into the mix, *this is why we can't have nice things.*

I mentioned earlier that God allowed the Israelites to plunder the treasures of Egypt before setting off on their exodus. Unfortunately, this treasure did not remain in their luggage but wormed its way into their hearts, corrupting their identity. A similar movement is what took place in the Garden of Eden. When mankind opened their hearts to hear the opinion of the serpent, those words of pride and deception did not merely pass through the ear canal and safely evaporate into nothing; rather, like a Morgul blade, they entered the very core of our being. One might say that our "FCH processing center" was pierced and corrupted. We call this event "the Fall," and it resulted in the cataclysmic rise of the sin nature, a very real state (the fatal fantastic element), which now exists to influence and distort the God-given cravings of our souls. God identifies the devastating result of this corruption when He speaks in Jeremiah 17:9, saying, "The heart is deceitful above all things."

And why Romans 13:10 so rightly declares, "No one is righteous, not even one."

Because of the Fall, we are now, by nature, self-deprecating, relentlessly flirting with "fatal rubbish."

HEAVENLY PROVISION

How do you love someone like that, someone who continuously pursues self-harm and folly? For most of us, we don't even try! We place as much distance between ourselves and the self-destructive personality as possible. But what if you *love* that self-destructive person? What if you are absolutely dedicated to never leaving or forsaking them? What then?

The most plausible solution might be incarceration. Lock them in a padded cell. Remove all opportunities for freedom and self-expression, knowing they would just do something evil with it anyway. That would be the easiest thing to do, perhaps even the most logical. The beauty (and the conundrum) of love, is that it is *not logical.* Love seeks to do the *good* thing, not the obvious or the easy thing. If you remove freedom and self-expression, you remove the opportunity for happiness, and that's not love.

It has been suggested that if you love someone, you need to let them go. I believe this to be at least partially true. It's *untrue* in that love, by its very nature, pursues and never gives up (1 Corinthians 13:7–8). But it *is* true in that love must also grant independence, or it robs its beneficiary of a crucial component necessary for the experience of true fulfillment.

So back to the question: *How do you love a self-destructive person?*

You teach them. You warn them. You have patience with them. You do what you can to implement safeguards, and you walk with them every step of the way. If they run off, you let them run off, but you never abandon them. You protect them from external attack, but you lovingly allow them to experience the consequences of their actions. At times, you show them sacrificial love, and at other times, tough love!

This is exactly what God has done for us! It's not the easy thing, but it is the good thing. For those who have not yet believed in His Name, He continues to pursue them patiently, yet *relentlessly*. He never abandons them!

For those who have recognized their sins and have turned to Jesus as the only Savior (the Healing Balm for their tainted souls), He releases them to pursue safe independence, beautifully guided and protected within the loving framework of His perfect Word. Under this protective Shield, they can explore and experiment without fear.

Our Heavenly Father invites us to pursue independence; to laugh, love, and create and to enjoy life as unique individuals. And on the occasions that God's Word forbids something, it is with love written all over it. The frequency with which I hear God say, "no" is in direct correlation with the level of my self-destructive mania.

To summarize, we are affectionately created and released to pursue independence *with* God, and *in* God; to these pursuits, God lends His full support. However, independence *from* God will ultimately result in our destruction, which is why He will not endorse it. In fact, independence from God is a fair definition for Hell itself.

> Hell: the absence of God; danger; confusion; the five core humanities insatiably desired, yet forever out of reach; eternal self-destruction.

Indeed, the torments of Hell will not derive from God! Rather, Hell is an approaching time and contain space, in which mankind (along with Satan and his minions) will be granted the opportunity to *fully* do things their way—without any restraint. Thus, the biblical descriptions of darkness, fire, and the gnashing of teeth can just as easily be viewed as *self-induced* agonies—agonies that God does not wish on anyone. Still, with great sadness, He will eventually grant these horrifying opportunities to the insistent and rebellious soul.

The counterfeit freedom the serpent offers arrogantly ignores God's safety barriers, predictably resulting in danger, and even death. Such an existence results in unfulfilled living under the bondage of fear. Jesus alone can overcome the sin nature and release us from this bondage. Truthfully, He *longs* to release us from this bondage. Galatians 5:1 triumphantly declares, "It is for freedom that Christ has set us free."

It is in the Word of Christ alone that we find a safe place to pursue our God-given craving for independence. All other ground is sinking sand. Not only does our Maker set us free to pursue a full and godly life, but He also created us to be distinct individuals. He knows your name! With love and purpose, He formed you in your mother's womb. There is no one quite like you, and it is with great kindness and love that God designed you this way.

DEAR HEAVENLY FATHER,

I THANK YOU FOR THE PROTECTION OF YOUR
ARMS, FOR NEVER LEAVING OR FORSAKING
ME, EVEN DESPITE MY SELF-DESTRUCTIVE
TENDENCIES. THANK YOU FOR DELIGHTING IN
VARIETY, FOR FINDING JOY IN WATCHING YOUR
CHILDREN GROW, AND FOR RELEASING US TO
EXPLORE THE MARVELS OF YOUR CREATION.
HOW WONDEROUS IT IS TO KNOW THAT THE
GOD OF THE UNIVERSE COULD DELIGHT IN ME!
STILL, EVEN IN THE FACE OF YOUR GOODNESS,
I HEAR THE SERPENT'S CALL TO WANDER,
SO I INVITE YOU TO BE THE MASTER OF MY
FEET: MY COMPASS AND MY GUIDE. LEAD
ME ALONG YOUR PATH, YOUR GOOD ROAD,
YOUR TRUE DIRECTION, YOUR SAFE HARBOR.
HELP ME IDENTIFY AND REJECT ANY SINFUL
DISTORTIONS MASQUERADING AS YOUR GOOD
DESIGN. AMEN.

INDEPENDENCE REFLECTION JOURNAL

- As an act of private confession, which of God's protective safety barriers have you most persistently pushed against?

- In accordance with the scriptures, what should repentance look like in this context?

- Can you identify (and celebrate) any ways in which God has blessed you with unique individuality?
  1. _____
  2. _____
  3. _____

- Without self-righteously judging someone else, is there anyone you can think of who may struggle with this specific craving? How can you use this fresh awareness to better understand and love them?

NOTES:

_____
_____
_____
_____
_____
_____
_____
_____
_____
_____
_____
_____
_____
_____
_____
_____
_____
_____

Chapter 7

1 AM SPECIAL!
(A CRAVING FOR SIGNIFICANCE)

I n our craving for independence, we desire something that sets us apart—but in our thirst for *significance*, we long for something that places us *above*. We need to know that we are not only unique but also special. This craving is the motivating force that drives us to excel, relentlessly propelling us toward achievement and success. It is also the root of both our destructive ego and our fear of failure (the fear of being unsuccessful and therefore, in our minds, of becoming insignificant).

At times, our craving for *security* or *identity* will create in us a want for camouflage, a covering that allows us to safely blend in with our surroundings—only to suddenly be upended by our desire for *independence* or *significance*, each boldly raising a neon banner and shouting, "Here I am! look at me!" Truly, we live much of our lives caught in the paradox of both wanting to be seen yet remain hidden. Finding a healthy balance in what can appear to be a titanic clash of cravings is necessary if we are to experience happiness and peace.

As much as any other core humanity, our craving for significance radically influences every aspect of our lives, and its audible cry can be heard in everything from the roar of a muscle car engine to the gentle hum of a stylist's sewing machine.

Consider this question: do we find significance in things that are valuable, or do we place value on things in accordance with their potential to make us feel significant? Probably both, but more the latter. For example, is Volkswagen *actually* the best brand of vehicle on the road? Or do I just *claim* it's the best because I drive one, and I want to feel significant about something?

Or we can flip the argument and ask, was the referee *actually* biased, or do I just *claim* he was biased because my team didn't win the game and, in losing, I don't feel significant? Again, at times it may be the first, but more often it's the latter.

Both as individuals and as cultures, we are quick to adjust our value metrics in an effort to maximize our ability to both gain and maintain a sense of significance. Historically, many of the objects or traits we value have remained consistent throughout time: strength, beauty, knowledge, success, ethic, position, and power. Yet we are very eager to redefine, reframe, or revise what we consider to *be* beautiful, ethical, wise, etc., should we determine that current definitions may be hindering our personal pursuit of the five core humanities.

Have you ever been playing a card or a board game with friends or family, when suddenly one of them urgently petitions for a rule change? You can bet they were seeking to gain an advantage or avoid a collapse. Similarly, we frequently witness this same petitioning taking place throughout the culture as a whole. If a certain group or individual feels they can't succeed under the current framework, they will eventually begin pushing for the implementation of new rules or special exceptions. When enough voices merge together in a unified call to revise a previously established social or economic parameter, it results in what we call *a cultural evolution* (or *revolution*, depending upon the method of change implemented). We are extremely serious about this adaptation, as it serves the fundamental purpose of enabling each new generation to attain and assert *their own* sense of security, identity, independence, significance, and innocence. History is full of both positive and negative examples regarding these cultural transformations.

In like manner, our craving for significance can be both beautiful and hideous, depending on where we direct it. At its best, it motivates us to create something dazzling. At its worst, it entices us toward malicious talk and jealousy; it tempts us to sully the reputation of others in a cheap effort to elevate ourselves. One thing is certain: when it comes to significance, we are all full-blown addicts.

AT ITS BEST

It takes hard work to become proficient at something. Construction, engineering, artistry, mathematics, you name it. Becoming skilled in any craft requires personal sacrifice and dedication. Our soul craving for significance is what pushes us to make this sacrifice in the pursuit of excellence.

Imagine how different it would be to live in a world where no one was motivated to do the hard work necessary to create something special. How drab would our music be? How colorless our art? How minimalist our architecture? How uninspired our worship? Much of what we call ingenuity or creativity simply wouldn't exist; each one of us would put in the minimum effort necessary to make something safe and functional. Thank goodness that isn't the case. Our innate craving for significance is what motivates us toward a higher level of growth, fulfillment, and achievement.

We are attracted to that which we deem to be significant. At its very best, this craving goads us toward hard work and creativity; it propels us toward beauty and inspires us toward betterment.

AT ITS WORST

Our need to feel significant (i.e., to be recognized as someone special) can often be what motivates ego, arrogance, and even the desire to control and dominate. My hunger for significance is what inspires me to reach for the stars—and be willing to step on your neck to get there. Sadly, many people conclude that the easiest route to feeling significant is not by growing as an individual but by diminishing, belittling, or subjugating others. For such people, significance isn't sought through reaching up but by pushing down. The tyrant, the bully, the cheat—they're all chasing significance (and probably a missing sense of security as well). At its worst, our craving for significance can lead us to devalue or even dehumanize others in a desperate attempt to elevate ourselves. Take a look around our society, even the local community, and you will see the effects of this everywhere.

We *all* desire the grand feeling of significance. This is why winning creates euphoria and losing stings. It's also why we humans are quick to move the goalposts, to change the rules or even the game, all in an effort to improve the odds of our success.

LESSONS FROM SATAN AND JESUS

Satan may be the most notorious example of a craving for significance gone wrong. The Bible is very clear regarding the schemes of Satan and even the promise of his ultimate demise, but our knowledge is limited as to his origins. We know God created him. We know he was likely an angel. There seems to be evidence that he led an angelic revolt against God and in response, God cast him out of Heaven. The result is that now, throughout the scriptures, Satan is identified as the very embodiment of evil. To be clear, God did not create this evil. God created something good, but like us, Satan experienced a fall. He, too, believed a lie, only in his case, it was his own lie.

Isaiah 14:13–14 testifies against Satan, stating,

> *You said in your heart,*
> *"I will ascend to the heavens;*
> *I will raise my throne*
> *above the stars of God;*
> *I will sit enthroned*
> *on the mount of assembly,*
> *on the utmost heights of Mount Zaphon.*
> *I will ascend above the tops of the clouds;*
> *I will make myself like the Most High."*

Satan wanted to rival God, and he became convinced he could achieve this goal. Of course, we know he failed, and in bitterness, he now roams the earth like a roaring lion. It should be noted that Satan's failure was inevitable. After all, Satan isn't omnipresent. He isn't omniscient. He isn't all-powerful. He doesn't transcend time and space. It's also worth noting that you and I don't either. Indeed, it is both a theological and scientific fact that God alone is capable of being God.

So what was the root cause of Satan's notorious downfall? What motivated him to foolishly attempt a celestial coup? Scripture is clear on this topic—it's an open-and-shut case of delusional *pride*, and pride is *often* rooted in the fanciful craving for counterfeit significance.

The reason Satan deceived Adam and Eve is that he had already deceived himself. Indeed, the lies we tell *ourselves* are the most potent of all lies, for their roots are sunk the deepest. Once we are persuaded by a lie, it naturally follows that we spread the deception as though it were the truth, having become convinced that it is. There are few people as dangerous (or as pitiful) as those who are convinced that lies are the truth or that truth is a lie, yet this delusion describes Satan in a nutshell. His mind is a tangled web of upside-down reasoning.

Throughout the pages of Scripture, Satan's actions appear like those of a madman, complete with self-deception, irrational choices, a massive ego, and blind rage. Sadly, mankind has been mimicking these same destructive actions throughout our tumultuous history. Satan's story, along with our own, are epic examples of the dire consequences experienced when we search for significance in counterfeit sources.

Jesus, of course, is the polar opposite of Satan. Jesus *is* omnipresent. He *is* omniscient. He *is* all-powerful. He *does* transcend time and space. He *is* God, so it comes as no surprise that Jesus would model the pursuit of significance in the exact *opposite* way that Satan did.

While Satan craved a dramatic promotion, Philippians 2:6–7 celebrates Christ, declaring,

> *Who, being in very nature God, did not consider equality with God something to be used to his own advantage; rather, he made himself nothing by taking the very nature of a servant, being made in human*

likeness. And being found in appearance as a man,
he humbled himself by becoming obedient to death—
even death on a cross!

The contrast between their modes of pursuit could not be more vast. I think we would all agree that the humility demonstrated by Jesus is both beautiful and good. But how is humility an efficient route to significance? At first glance, humility would appear to be a route that is both painful and slow. In fact, many have come to that exact conclusion. However, look at the passage that immediately follows:

Therefore God exalted him to the highest place and
gave him the name that is above every name, that at
the name of Jesus every knee should bow, in heaven
and on earth and under the earth, and every tongue
acknowledge that Jesus Christ is Lord (Philippians
2:9–11).

Through the act of humility, Jesus *transcended* mere significance, and He is now considered to be the *most* significant—*above everything!* This principle also applies to us. Matthew 23:12 teaches,

For those who exalt themselves will be humbled, and
those who humble themselves will be exalted.

And then, in 1 Peter 5:5–6,

All of you, clothe yourselves with humility toward one
another, because, "God opposes the proud but shows

favor to the humble." Humble yourselves, therefore,
under God's mighty hand, that he may lift you up.

God Himself elevates the humble—and *exalts* them. That's
amazing! It makes perfect sense for us to exalt God, but for God
to exalt us? It's astonishing—delightfully so. Doing things God's
way is always the most efficient and the most rewarding.

HEAVENLY PROVISION

It's important we do not reach the conclusion that significance
is only realized in our "good behaviors"—even a behavior as beautiful as humility. Such a conclusion would place Christianity upon
the same cumbersome plane as the world and its eclectic collection
of works-based religions. Indeed, our *greatest* awareness of significance is not discovered in what we do, but in embracing who God
says we are. So who are you?

- You are a child of the King of kings and Lord of lords, the
  crown jewel of creation!
- You are a joint heir with Christ, lovingly and uniquely
  created in the image of God!
- You are an individual of such immense value that He, the
  Master of the universe, allowed Himself to be savagely
  beaten. He, the Immortal One, willingly died on the cross
  to save your soul!

Significance is not something we need to frantically pursue;
rather, it's something we experience when we take God at His
Word. We *have not*, and *cannot*, earn this high station in the heart
of God, yet it is our privileged position nonetheless.

The world is seeking significance through its achievements, through its "advancements," or through the social pecking order. But the reality is that each of our earthly works will fade and decay. Our towers will fall, our digital servers will short out, and our statues will crumble or melt in the heat. Eventually, all earthly deeds will be forgotten, all save those divinely preserved so they might continue to teach us this valuable lesson.

Meaningful satisfaction *does not exist* in temporal and fallible sources. From a certain perspective, it seems as though the world has begrudgingly accepted this truth through a Freudian slip. Increasingly, we hear phrases like, "The joy is in the chase." In other words, it is generally acknowledged that all this running about isn't actually getting people anywhere, and so, predictably, the metric is revised. Now *the pursuit* is considered to be the most significant aspect of living. What an exhausting thought: running for running's sake! Ugh! Still, it is commonplace today to hear someone say, "Life is about the journey, not the destination." The problem with this concept is that sooner or later, we all get tired or discouraged, and we can't move another step. What then?

Ultimately, this *chase philosophy* offers little more than a lifelong death march. It's the serpent's attempt at a pep talk, one purposefully designed to brainwash us into enthusiastically chasing after emptiness. Similar to the mirage of water in a parched desert, his slithering lies motivate us to pursue a distant provision that never materializes. But according to the snake, we shouldn't worry about this because "the joy is in the chase?" Personally, I'm not buying what the serpent is selling, though many others have. Not surprisingly, this metaphorical desert is now littered with the gaunt and shriveled bodies of the spiritually malnourished.

Thankfully, this does not have to be our fate. The apostle Paul triumphantly declares in 1 Corinthians 9:26, "I do not run like someone running aimlessly."

The same can be said of all who follow Christ. We run with purpose, equipped with abundant provisions, as we embrace both the adventure *and* the *rest* of the Father's heart.

Your pursuit of significance does not need to resemble an unending game of one-upmanship—a chase, a competition, or a grueling journey. Neither does it need to be fraudulently imagined in the frailty of your mind. Your significance is *real, accessible, available,* and *secure.* If you listen, even now, you will hear the Lord of heaven and earth saying, "I have loved you with an everlasting love" (Jeremiah 31:3). All you have to determine is whether or not you believe Him!

You *are* significant! Christ has shown you the proof through the nail scars in His hands.

DEAR HEAVENLY FATHER,

PLEASE FORGIVE ME FOR MY FOOLISH WANDERINGS, FOR PURSUING SIGNIFICANCE THAT I MIGHT BOOST MY OWN EGO AND SERVE MY OWN DELUSIONS. WHEN I REALIZE THE VALUE YOU HAVE PLACED UPON ME, I CAN'T HELP BUT MARVEL AT THE VAST MEASURE OF YOUR INCOMPREHENSIBLE KINDNESS. THOUGH I DON'T FULLY UNDERSTAND IT, I WANT TO THANK YOU FOR YOUR TENDERNESS TOWARD ME. I RECEIVE IT AND CLING TO IT. I AM SIGNIFICANT BECAUSE YOU HAVE DECLARED ME TO BE, AND FOR THAT, I AM BOTH HUMBLED AND THANKFUL. AMEN.

SIGNIFICANCE REFLECTION JOURNAL

- If you are honest with yourself, where have you primarily been searching for worldly significance? (Circle any that apply to your circumstance.)

Career/Achievement	Fantasy
Power/Authority	Finances/Possessions
Social Affirmation	Knowledge/Education
Relationships	Other (explain)
Winning	

- What does God want you to know about His feelings toward you in this regard?

- Is there anyone you have diminished, belittled, or subjugated in the pursuit of worldly significance? Can you summon the courage to ask for forgiveness? YES or NO. (I understand that this is a tough one.)

- Without self-righteously judging someone else, is there anyone you can think of who may struggle with this specific craving? How can you use this fresh awareness to better understand and love them?

NOTES:

Chapter 8

I'M A GOOD PERSON!
(A CRAVING FOR INNOCENCE)

Whatever you do, don't underestimate the power and influence of your craving for innocence! There are few things capable of stabilizing or destabilizing your home and your heart faster than this incessant craving. Both in the positive and the negative sense, our craving for innocence has a huge impact on all human interaction.

Pointed in the right direction, we are driven to actually *be* innocent: to follow the law, to honor our commitments, and to do the "right thing." When this craving is on track, it motivates us toward decency, kindness, and fair play.

Conversely, if pointed in the *wrong direction*, my craving for innocence will tempt me to shift blame, deflect accusations, abdicate personal responsibility, or insist that any negative action on my part was a justified reaction to something terrible that "you did first." It's childish, yes; it's also profoundly human.

THE FRUSTRATION OF NEUTRALITY

I specifically remember the frustration I experienced in middle school regarding Jason Roberts. Jason was an extremely nice person and a friend. He was thoughtful, kind, academically gifted, and the *obvious* teacher's pet. My frustration with him made no sense at all—apart from my jealousy. My jealousy was primarily based on the high level of positive attention he received: positive attention that I was *not* receiving.

I did not rank among the problem kids, but neither was I categorized alongside "Saint Jason." I was placed in the periphery, marginalized by normalcy. Existing in this neutral position felt akin to living in no-man's land, and I found it to be quietly yet *deeply* frustrating.

This frustration over neutrality is very apropos when it comes to our innocence craving. Being identified as *not a bad person* is not enough—we long to be considered *good* people. The difference between a "not bad person" and a "good person" is vast: one (me) is considered "not guilty" while the other (Jason) is considered *righteous*. "Not guilty" will do in a pinch, but ultimately, we are craving something more.

Perhaps it is just the natural progression of the craving, or perhaps it happens when our need for innocence melds with our need for significance. Either way, we tend to crave an *excess of innocence*, culminating in a euphoric sense of personal holiness.

While modern culture increasingly seeks to marginalize religious thought and practice, it has by no means lost its enthusiasm to feel self-righteous and harshly judge any "sinner" it finds guilty of breaking newly formed social rules. One thing is certain: as with faith, piety is not exclusive to organized religion. For both the believer and the unbeliever alike, righteousness feels really, really good, and we witness the active pursuit of its bounty throughout every level of our society.

A HYPERSENSITIVITY

Truly, the profound influence of this "righteousness" or "rightness" aspect of our craving cannot be overstated. Over the years, I have counseled many people who had become convinced (to a crippling degree) that their *personal worth* was directly linked to their sense of rightness. In their minds, if they were proven to be incorrect in any way, they translated it to mean they were *guilty* of an extreme violation, and therefore, they were without worth! This high level of sensitivity made even the smallest of disagreements taste just as bitter as unjust accusations, and it eventually placed a great deal of stress on their closest relationships, as mere differences in opinion quickly escalated into titanic battles for self-worth. Sadly, this hypersensitivity regarding guilt and innocence is often rooted in a childhood experience that was filled with repetitive accusations or performance-based affection.

The *right-equals-worth* perspective is not uncommon. Deep down, we each hold a similar view, though we clearly appear at different points on the spectrum. Those among us who have gained a reputation for being particularly argumentative or defensive are often those who struggle with this destructive self-imaging.

No doubt you are familiar with the adage "live and let live" or "just let it go," and these statements sound wise ... until we realize that implementing their wisdom will require us to find happiness while being fully aware that certain individuals believe us to be bad or wrong. This is hard for most of us, as our craving to both *feel innocent* and have others *believe we are good* compels us to passionately plead our case, incessantly defending ourselves. This can be exhausting, not just on a relational level, but in the very soul.

Living or working with someone who is constantly accusing you of attacking them, or who is regularly attacking *your* sense of innocence, is a disaster. It's no way to live, and it may be the single biggest cause of strained relationships. And yet, as previously mentioned, it doesn't only affect personal relationships, but potentially entire cultures.

Today, we live in what has been dubbed a "cancel culture," a culture that offers very little forgiveness and which seems poised to pounce on you for even the slightest perceived transgression (regardless of whether that transgression took place five minutes or twenty years ago). A distorted sense of the innocence/righteousness metric has played a major role in the cultivation and growth of this stressful environment. Without question, our insatiable craving for innocence dramatically impacts both our personal and social existence. And things can become downright messy when your craving begins to collide with those around you.

DISTORTED INNOCENCE

When our craving for innocence is distorted, it becomes hostile and defensive. Consider this: basically every argument you've ever had, or any offense you've ever taken, was triggered by someone subtly or aggressively insinuating that you were guilty of wrongdoing or wrong thinking. They claimed you didn't speak or behave in a manner that you should have. Your likely response was to defend your innocence, to shift the blame for your guilt, or to push back and accuse the other person of greater wrongdoing. In the heat of the moment, it is not necessary to feel *totally* innocent; you simply need to believe you are *less* guilty than they are. Thus, the twisted competition begins, and the righteousness metric is invoked: who is the *most* innocent?

We often pursue this fraudulent sense of moral dominance by amplifying the vice of others while simultaneously minimizing their virtues. We then compare them against our own amplified virtues and minimized vices, thus producing a skewed and dishonest assessment. What was intended to be a good and godly craving suddenly becomes delusional, self-serving, and militant. It mirrors a twisted sense of significance in that we are similarly tempted to satisfy our craving by tearing others down rather than by personally reaching up.

Our craving for innocence was designed to be a beautiful and connective force, a happy pressure motivating us toward right action and peaceful living. But as a distortion, it is notoriously selfish, often manifesting as a relentless victim mentality. It wreaks havoc through incessant defensiveness, accusation, and self-righteousness.

Identifying a victim-driven mentality in someone else is easy (we find it aggravating, deceptive, unadmirable, and exhausting), but it's much more challenging to acknowledge it within ourselves. Why is that? Why is it so hard to acknowledge our own transgressions and mistakes, even to ourselves? (Sometimes *especially* to ourselves!)

Answer: If I admit that I exhibit the same unadmirable behaviors that I despise in others, then I am admitting guilt and hypocrisy, and there are few things we humans find as vile as a guilty hypocrite. To acknowledge this hard truth about ourselves is a massive gut punch to our craving for innocence, and so our *sin nature* springs forward to activate a self-defense mechanism, one that "protects us" from the honest awareness of our own guilt. It deploys a metaphorical blindfold, specifically designed to hide me from myself. Once activated, I can clearly see the speck of dust in my neighbor's eye (in fact, the speck is generally exaggerated), but I am now oblivious to the log in my eye. Please note that it is our *sin nature* that activates this mechanism, which, in typical serpent fashion, always has the opposite effect than it claims it will have.

A healthy craving for innocence helps us recognize when we have gone off track, and it implements a course correction. It inspires apology, behavior adjustment, and the desire to make restitution. Distorted innocence has no such corrective interests—and so a crash is imminent.

> A HEALTHY CRAVING FOR INNOCENCE HELPS US RECOGNIZE WHEN WE HAVE GONE OFF TRACK, AND IT IMPLEMENTS A COURSE CORRECTION.

The tragic distorting of this core humanity will eventually create an anti-utopian society, an environment in which a statement as simple as "You left your socks on the floor again, honey" can quickly escalate into a relationship-ending dispute.

If we feel we are being accused, shamed, or blamed in any way, our fallen human instinct is either to turn and run or to push back hard. Sadly, those of us who do not learn to manage our craving for innocence in a healthy manner will eventually leave a trail of broken relationships behind us, and in classic Eden fashion, we will blame everyone but ourselves.

THE DREAD PARADOX

You may be at the zenith of your career, experiencing a season of life overflowing with a bounty of security, identity, independence, and significance; but if someone or something is triggering a sense of guilt, you will experience an insatiable desire to fight or flee. This is true for all of us. The craving for innocence exists in every human soul, and how we manage it will have a profound impact, not merely on our personal quality of life, but on our communal quality of life as well.

God, in His perfect wisdom, designed this craving as a good and beautiful attribute. It motivates all human decency, and it faithfully seeks to place us in right standing with both our neighbor and our Maker. And yet our sin nature has created a dreadful paradox. As members of the human race, we are no strangers to paradox living, and the innocence/guilt paradox stands second to none. On the one hand, we desperately crave innocence, yet on the other, we perpetually misbehave, so much so that 1 John 1:8 says,

> *If we claim to be without sin,*
> *we deceive ourselves and the truth is not in us.*

The individual who claims to be without sin has had the blindfold activated by the sin nature. Such ignorance is not bliss. In fact, it will eventually crescendo in calamity. Always remember, everything the serpent suggests is the *opposite* of reality, which is why his self-defense mechanism predictably results in self-destruction and why his truth always culminates in a lie.

The apostle Paul may have described life in the paradox best when, in Romans 7:19, he laments,

> *For I do not do the good I want to do,*
> *but the evil I do not want to do—this I keep on doing.*

Paul wrote these words almost two thousand years ago, and we can still identify with them today. They describe the reality of *all* of us. My craving for innocence compels me to *want* to do what is right—but my sin nature effectively diverts me into folly! Frustration and desperation boil over in verse 24 as Paul shouts, "What a wretched man I am! Who will rescue me from this body?"

HEAVENLY PROVISION

Paul's "wretched man" monologue is a brutal yet honest assessment of each one of us (as marred by sin), and his question is one of vital importance. Our craving for innocence is consuming, *intentionally so*, and yet our inability to properly behave for any length of time is desperately frustrating! Of all our paradoxes, this is the worst! So what is the answer to Paul's question? *Who will save me?*

Thankfully, delightfully, Paul bursts forth with the answer in verse 25: "Thanks be to God, who delivers me through Jesus Christ our Lord!"

Jesus is the answer! *He* delivers us from the clutches of the paradox.

The day will come when we reach our heavenly home, and the great burden of our sin nature will forever be removed from our backs and eradicated. The scales will fully drop from our eyes, and the distortions will come to an end. In the meantime, while we await the return of our Lord, the Gospel of Jesus Christ extends a hope-filled message to the whole world. We call it the Good News, and its daily relevance applies to both the lost *and* the found. If you are already a Christ follower, don't think for a second that this message no longer applies to you. Don't let the Good News become old news, and don't allow the stress of the paradox to creep back into your life! You are delivered. It is finished!

The joy of the Gospel held out in Colossians 2:13–14 still applies, even after repeated failure.

When you were dead in your sins and in the uncir-
cumcision of your flesh, God made you alive with
Christ. He forgave us all our sins, having canceled the
charge of our legal indebtedness, which stood against
us and condemned us; he has taken it away, nailing
it to the cross.

This celebration continues in Romans 8:1, "There is now no condemnation for those who are in Christ Jesus."

Freedom! Forgiveness! Redemption! Reconciliation! The answer to the paradox! This is why we call Him the Savior! This is why the scriptures are filled with phrases like "Praise the Lord!" "Hallelujah!" "Glory to the Most High!"

Jesus is the answer! In fact, our craving for innocence was *designed* to draw us toward the protection of His everlasting arms, a place in which the paradox holds no power or sway. Still, deception and distortion lie in wait along the pilgrim trail. We must therefore remain alert and sober-minded.

DOUBLE-BARRELED DISTORTIONS

Our sin nature promotes a distorted sense of innocence, one that in true self-deprecating fashion seeks to crush us in two primary ways:

- Distortion no. 1 seeks to drag us into despair by convincing us there is no hope, that we are so guilty, so unlovable, so sinful that we are worth nothing!

- Distortion no. 2 tries to convince us that we are innocent (though we clearly are not). It fills us with indignant self-righteousness, and it blinds us to ourselves.

As an act of artistic license, I will henceforth refer to distortion no. 1 as *Mr. Despair* and to distortion no. 2 as *Lil' Miss Indignant*.

Many of us have witnessed those trapped and entangled by Mr. Despair, and it breaks our hearts. The old miser holds his boot of shame against the throat of the weary soul, resulting in humiliation and self-loathing. Thankfully, the church has done a decent job in reaching out to those held hostage by Mr. Despair, breaking their chains with the message of hope and validation found only in Jesus Christ. To quote Betsie ten Boom, "There is no pit so deep that God's love is not deeper still"; and before the power of this great love, Mr. Despair must flee in terror. That said, there is much work yet to be done. Mr. Despair is an expert in secrecy, so we must maintain a sharp and discerning lookout for those trapped in bondage and servitude to his soul-crushing lies.

Lil' Miss Indignant, however, is a different matter altogether. The modern church finds her intimidating and is often confused about what to do with her. She is flamboyant, charismatic, and in your face. Additionally, she is highly educated and self-righteous. She also boasts a huge social media following, making her an ideal candidate for book deals and television appearances.

Most church fellowships have a strong desire to be viewed as a positive influence in their community, but Lil' Miss Indignant throws that hope right back in their faces, hurling accusations and even threatening retaliation. Nor are her threats hollow. She has personally led the charge to intimidate, silence, and cancel many.

Unlike Mr. Despair, Lil' Miss Indignant is *actively* hostile toward the gospel, and for good reason: the gospel demands her complete and unequivocal surrender; it exposes her for the fraud she is!

A foundational tenet of the Christian faith is repentance, the honest confession of sin (which is really the confession of truth).

This act of humble repentance opens a holy valve of blessing, releasing a bountiful supply of forgiveness, redemption, and grace, all flowing from the Cross of Christ. This happy flood washes over us, cleansing the sinful soul and presenting us to God as innocent, free from accusation, and justified through the work of Christ Jesus. But Lil' Miss Indignant feels no need for repentance nor redemption, and she thereby views the gospel as hostile, derogatory, and oppressive. While Mr. Despair flees in fear before the gospel, Lil' Miss Indignant rallies increasingly powerful forces against it.

To the individual who vehemently takes their stand alongside Lil' Miss Indignant, I can offer no help save the continued exposition of truth and intercessory prayer. Truth and prayer are of great help indeed, as they unleash both the unfailing Word of God and the Holy Spirit—more than enough divine power to awaken the slumbering soul, even the hostile one. To that end, I continue to pray for a great wave of revelation and defection to sweep through the deceiver's camp.

We are all craving innocence, yet these two distortions purvey soul-crushing lies, lies employed by the serpent to misdirect and discourage. As believers, we ought to dispatch these distortions from our God-given spheres of influence with the utmost prejudice, nailing them to the cross of Calvary.

Jesus offers us a better paradox, a happy one, one that can save our souls and bring peace. The paradox is this: only in the honest confession of guilt can we be declared fully innocent! Jesus is the gatekeeper to this opportunity. He's opening the gate for you even now. Will you walk through?

DEAR LORD,

I COME TO YOU AND CONFESS MY GUILT. I HAVE SOUGHT MY INNOCENCE IN COUNTERFEIT AND DISTORTION. I HAVE PLACED MY WORTH IN HOLLOW SELF-RIGHTEOUSNESS, AND I NOW SEE HOW I HAVE HURT OTHERS IN THIS VAIN PURSUIT. I ASK YOUR FORGIVENESS, LORD. I PLEAD FOR YOUR MERCY. THANK YOU FOR YOUR BOUNTIFUL PROVISION OF GRACE TO WHICH I HAVE SO LONG BEEN BLIND. I ASK THAT YOU HELP ME TEAR THESE BLINDERS OFF MY EYES, THAT I MIGHT SEE YOUR GOODNESS IN ITS VAST IMMEASURABLE DISPLAY. THANK YOU FOR NAILING MY GUILT TO THE CROSS, THAT I MIGHT WALK IN YOUR INNOCENCE AND BE COVERED IN YOUR RIGHTEOUSNESS. AMEN.

INNOCENCE REFLECTION JOURNAL

- What strategy does your sin nature most often employ in the pursuit of distorted innocence? (Circle any that apply to your circumstance.)

Defensiveness	Lying
Lawyering	Denial
Retaliatory Accusation	All of the Above

What can you do to become healthy in this area?

1. _____
2. _____
3. _____

- Who are you more familiar with?
  - Mr. Despair
  - Lil' Miss Indignant
  - They generally take turns tag-teaming me

- What can you do about it?

1. _____
2. _____
3. _____

- Without self-righteously judging someone else, is there anyone you can think of who may struggle with this specific craving? How can you use this fresh awareness to better understand and love them?

NOTES:

Part 2

THE PATHWAY TO PEACE

Chapter 9

THE MOUNTAINTOP

Having made it this far, you have now been introduced to the five core cravings of your soul. You know these cravings by name, and hopefully, you feel better equipped to address their needs.

SECURITY—IDENTITY—INDEPENDENCE—
SIGNIFICANCE—INNOCENCE

They are innate and hardwired, the source of our every motivation. This is why we call them *humanities*. They are beautiful gifts forged by God Himself; though we have not always stewarded them in a wise and worthy manner. Some of us have sought fulfillment for these yearnings within our small everyday nouns (local people, places, and things), while others have pursued a larger stage: fame, notoriety, a literal larger stage. Our responses to unfulfilled cravings have also varied. Some of us have felt melancholy and defeated. Others have entered deep depression. Anger, anxiety, irritability, isolationism, and desperate ambition, all may be viewed as the psychological equivalent to hunger pains; your soul has been telling you it requires nourishment. What we are ultimately longing for is *peace*, that precious point of existence where all fears are stilled and every craving is satisfied. This is what the entire world is searching for.

NEED AND WANT

God created our core humanities for a wondrous purpose. Like iron to a magnet, they seek to draw each of us home to the cooperative identity of our Heavenly Father. The sin nature (that slithering foe since long ages of antiquity) stands in opposition to this happy reunion, relentlessly working to interrupt the magnetic pull by redirecting our God-given cravings toward self-destructive and counterfeit sources. Amid this conflict, teeming with our willful gullibility and habitual failure, it becomes apparent that God's *grace* is unquestionably our primary need. *Peace*, however, remains our highest want. The wonderful news is that God, in His goodness, has graciously granted provision for both need and want.

Providentially, almost every epistle begins with this prayer for us: "Grace and Peace be yours in abundance" (1 Peter 1:2, as one example).

This beautiful and repetitive supplication is made throughout the scriptures, with the blessing being directed toward you and me. Grace and peace—our greatest need and highest want! Is this prayer a coincidence? I think not! But how do we access such holistic provision? How do we make abundant grace and peace our *living reality*? We need clear answers, as both our temporal and eternal happiness are hinged upon them.

AMAZING GRACE

Because of our inherent and willful sin, every member of the human race is solely reliant on God's grace for salvation. It's important to note that we are not helpless victims of the sin nature, but willing collaborators. Just as the betrayal of adultery will drive a wedge between a husband and a wife, so also our dalliance with sin drives a wedge between God and ourselves. *We* are the breakers of faith and fellowship, rejecting God's goodness and choosing depravity. Lies, profanity, malice, gossip, pride, selfishness, perversion: I do not pronounce these judgments lightly. I grieve deeply, recognizing the vast measure of my own guilt. Then into my guilt and grief enters the unimaginable love of Christ, beautifully bent on saving me from myself! *I* am the betrayer and the adulterer—*the guilt is mine*! Yet Jesus steps forward to pay my debt. This is our story! This is our song! The mystery of the incarnation, the terror of the cross, the glory of the empty tomb, the power of the Holy Spirit sent to guard and to guide—we (*even as the perpetrators*) are the beneficiaries of incomprehensible kindness.

Still, holy justice demands a high penalty for our sins. The penalty of toil, fear, and ultimately, of death! Amazingly, Jesus takes my punishment upon Himself, paying my penalty in full. With nail-scarred hands of grace, He reaches out, extending the offer of eternal pardon. This mighty gift is freely offered, and it must be freely received.

So how does the sin/grace exchange work? How do I receive this good gift? To summarize the scriptures regarding salvation, we receive saving grace from God through the following:

- Recognizing our need to be saved
- Truly repenting of our sins
- Crying out to God for mercy
- Trusting and following Jesus as our Savior and Lord

These four actions are the substance of what the Bible calls *faith*, and through this faith we receive grace, resulting in the redemption of our souls. This blessed redemption reestablishes our peace with God. At this point, the eternal soul is marked safe from the clutches of death and Hell, and it joyfully awaits its heavenly home.

BASE CAMP VS. THE SUMMIT

I would be doing you a disservice if I didn't point out that having peace *with* God is altogether different from experiencing peace *in* God. I do not think it heresy to lament the fact that we too often end our journey at the point of judicial peace, and we seldom press into the *living peace* found in relational communion with the Maker of our souls. This premature stoppage can often result in a distant and even *awkward* relationship with God—similar to a legally established marriage that is devoid of intimacy. It is no small wonder, then, why many Christians experience the frustration of discontentment. But God never intended us to camp at the judicial level of relationship, let alone build most of our churches there.

If I may use a mountaineering analogy, it would be like beginning the wondrous climb up the slopes of the highest and most glorious of all mountains (let's call it Mount de Paz), only to abruptly end our journey in a tent at base camp. Pausing at base camp is vitally important, to be certain. Having lived in the lowlands of sin for so long, our lungs now need time to adjust to the pure mountain air. But eventually, we ought to begin our push toward the joy of the Summit.

Unfortunately, many Christians spend their entire lives in the tent at base camp, casting a periodic gaze toward the high peak, their heart rate quickening at the thought of glorious adventure—only to release a somber sigh and turn once again to the familiarity of their cot. Such individuals sing songs of the Mighty Mountain; they name their churches after its majestic pinnacles, even inviting their friends to join them at base camp. But sooner or later, this static religious lifestyle can feel monotonous and boring. At this point, fine Christians who began their journey with sincere enthusiasm can often become discouraged and unhappy. Some make the regressive decision to return to the smog-filled valley below, while others attempt to spice up camp monotony through legalism, or by embroiling themselves in inter-camp conflicts. This is a spiritual tragedy, one that was never intended.

> AT THIS POINT, FINE CHRISTIANS WHO BEGAN THEIR JOURNEY WITH SINCERE ENTHUSIASM CAN OFTEN BECOME DISCOURAGED AND UNHAPPY.

Establishing peace *with* God is a nonnegotiable necessity; still, God's greatness is such that peace *with* Him can be likened to base camp, and He desires *even more* for us than this. He purposefully designed our souls to experience peace *in* Him—that's the Summit, where perfect peace resides. But it requires that we brave the cliffs, pressing onward and upward.

Unlike our earthly mountains, Mount de Paz is not capped with snow, ice, and frigid temperatures. Rather, upon its glorious heights we discover the temperate meadows of peace, soaring high above every earthly fear.

PATHWAY TO PEACE

So, how do we experience peace? I'm specifically referring to that *inner peace* that every member of the human race is actively craving. Analogies and homilies have their benefit, but there comes a point when we need to leave the metaphors behind and speak in plain language, so here it is (I encourage you to read it twice):

> *Perfect peace is only experienced when our core humanities are satisfied simultaneously.*

Sadly, this is the reason why our moments of peace are so fleeting. You may feel free from accusation and secure in your relationships, but if you are fearful that someone is attempting to hack into your bank account, you will not have peace. You may feel safe in your home and free to come and go as you please, but if you don't know who you are or whether there is a purpose to your existence, you will not have peace. If satisfaction for *even one* of these cravings is missing from our lives, it upsets the whole balance. Perfect peace is *only* experienced when the core cravings of our soul are satisfied *simultaneously!*

But there is nothing on earth that can grant such an experience in any lasting measure. Still, we have witnessed the world in their failed attempts to fill this God-shaped void with the *usual suspects*.

THE USUAL SUSPECTS

For thousands of years, mankind has sought fulfillment through **wealth**, **power**, and **fame**. I'm sure that all of us, at some point, have fantasized about joining the ranks of the rich and famous, imagining their glamorous lifestyles to be carefree and contented. Of course, a simple look into the *actual* lives of those who have gained this elite position in society quickly reveals that celebrity *does not* bring peace. Nonetheless, we all dream of the opportunity to prove ourselves the exception to the rule.

Plato and Aristotle then popularized the theory that peace and fulfillment could be obtained through **virtue, morality**, and personal **piety**. Without question, right living *is* praiseworthy and *very* appealing to our cravings for innocence, significance, and identity. Unfortunately, our pride, vanity, anger, and petty jealousies have always derailed any and all attempts to gain lasting peace through personal righteousness.

Next we have **freedom** and **connectedness**. We mistakenly presume that possessing limitless freedom will bring us peace—but it never has. In fact, a lack of boundaries often *wounds* and *exposes* us. As to connectedness, mankind has steadily promoted the idea that if we would just put aside our differences and gather together in a spirit of harmony, we could create heaven on earth. Regrettably, it's not that simple. If all our disagreements and distinctions were superficial, then maybe it would be a possibility. We could negotiate, compromise, forgive, and move forward together. However, the truth is many of our differences are *substantial*, relating to the foundational tenets of morality, safety, and overall worldview. In these cases, there can be no unity without one side suppressing or annihilating the other. Connectedness is not a realistic path to bliss—not while here on earth.

Then, of course, we have the pursuit of pleasure and peace through **sex** and **mind-altering substances**. The problem here is that it's never enough. These desperate choices ultimately bring real harm and potentially rob us of our innocence. They are self-debasing, serving only to numb the very pain God wants to fully heal.

Finally, there are the suspects of **denial** and **delusion**. What if we just deny the existence of truth? What if we imagine that everything is relative, and *we* are the definers of reality? Will this eliminate the strain of expectation and quiet our restlessness? No, it won't. We cannot deny and deceive our way into fulfillment and peace. No matter how hard we may try to delude ourselves, the Truth of God is living and active, and the Spirit of God faithfully and relentlessly reminds us that *more than deception* is available. Delusion won't work because God won't abandon us to such a pathetic fate.

Throughout the ages, mankind has repeatedly returned to these *usual suspects* without success. Yet for some strange, obsessional reason, we keep thinking our next effort will be enough.

MORE IS NOT ENOUGH

This brings us to one of our favorite topics: *more.*

I vividly remember making $12 an hour and being convinced, "If I can just make $15 an hour, I will finally be able to acquire everything I need to be happy." Then the day came when I was making $15 an hour, and suddenly, I revised the metric. Now I needed $20 to be happy! Then $30! My metric meddling continued for many years, and I, like everyone else, kept sensing that I needed "just a little bit more."

As a lifelong student of human behavior, I used to wonder if it wasn't our hunger for *more* that reigned as the king of all our cravings. After all, when you observe the people around you, more seems to be the clearly intended goal. For example, when wealth doesn't bring us peace, we generally conclude that we need to accumulate *more* wealth. When power doesn't equate to peace, we predictably assume we require *more* power.

Truly, mankind is less creative than we like to imagine, and this obsessive-compulsive mentality now permeates every aspect of our lives. We find ourselves craving more vacation days, more recognition, more sex, more respect, more sleep, more pairs of shoes, longer life, and so on and so forth. I have since come to believe that our craving for more is simply the soul's desperate response regarding its inability to find anything on earth that satisfies. *More* is not an original craving; it is merely the outworking of FCH desperation—like a drowning man sinking into the depths and frantically reaching for another handful of water to cling to.

MORE IS NOT AN ORIGINAL CRAVING; IT IS MERELY THE OUTWORKING OF FCH DESPERATION—LIKE A DROWNING MAN SINKING INTO THE DEPTHS AND FRANTICALLY REACHING FOR ANOTHER HANDFUL OF WATER TO CLING TO.

This same desperation has been heating up throughout society at an alarming rate of increase, and the reasoning behind the sudden temperature spike is not complicated. Our modern generation has gained access to *more* wealth, *more* leisure, *more* education, *more* freedom, *more* opportunity, *more* comfort, and *more* entertainment than any other generation in the history of the world—and still we have not found peace. We've climbed to the top of all the wrong mountains, and painfully discovered nothing there. We were *so confident* that a new relationship, a fresh achievement, a more profitable career, or a euphoric experience would grant us lasting peace ... but it has let us down. Today's culture is now grappling with the shock of this realization, and our collective desperation is nearing the boiling point. Sadly, mankind's fallen instinct has not been to return to God; rather, we obsessively restart the same hopeless cycle of injecting ever higher doses of the same failed medications.

This is the verdict: The world *fiercely* craves peace but increasingly marginalizes the God of peace. They crave a mountaintop experience but purposefully avoid the greatest Mountain of them all. The irony of this situation would be amusing if it wasn't so tragic and heartbreaking. This is why awakening to the cravings of our soul is of such high importance. Only in understanding what we're truly looking for do we have any hope of searching in the right direction.

HEAVENLY PROVISION

Peace is the culmination of everything we desire. It's what we strive for in our every pursuit—and it is only experienced when the cravings of our soul are satisfied simultaneously. Jesus, the Prince of Peace, the Creator and Sustainer of all things, is the *only One* who can make this peace a reality.

- He who conquered death and Hell is the only true source of *security*.
- Being made in His image, He is the very embodiment of our *identity*.
- Only within the protective framework of His perfect Word can we experience the joyful exploration of safe *independence*.
- Considering the magnitude of God and the incomprehensible value He places on *your* soul, there exists no greater sense of *significance* than realized in the depths of His love.
- Finally, we have the Cross and the empty tomb, the work of Christ, and the only true source of legitimate *innocence*.

Contrary to the ever-popular *usual suspects*; once you receive abundant life in Christ, you never need more. He is enough! His strength is enough. His grace is enough. His love is enough. His promise is enough.

Your Heavenly Father is calling you out of the rat race and into the fulfillment of His presence. From one soul to another, I implore you—heed His voice and *leave the proverbial rat race!* Take the words off this page and put them into glorious practice. If you're halfway up the wrong mountain, turn around. You'll gain nothing by advancing forward in an errant direction. In such an instance, your willingness to turn back is what will move you forward.

Jesus is the answer to our soul's craving. Only in relationship with our Maker can we experience the dual blessings of both perfect rest and glorious adventure. Even now, the magnetic heart of God is drawing your soul toward this pinnacle of Divine peace, and even now, your sin nature is attempting to deflect and distort.

Just as Homer's *Sirens* attempted to lure Odysseus off mission and into catastrophe, the sin nature is likewise working to divert your holy push toward the Summit of Mount de Paz and into an unholy wilderness of delusion. Thankfully, God will never leave you or forsake you. Even if your path leads through the valley of the shadow of death, if you continue to listen to the Savior's voice, you need fear no evil.

In the upcoming chapter, we will encounter the happy shadow of our Heavenly Father, and learn how to lean on each other in our united pursuit of peace.

Dear Lord,

I thank You, not only for Your gift of grace but also for Your bountiful provision of peace. I pray I would walk in it, that I would take my stand on its firm foundation. I thank You for mercies that are new every morning. I ask You help me recognize counterfeits for what they are. Give me a discerning heart; grant me eyes that spiritually see and ears that spiritually hear. I pray I would never become ignorant of the Devil's plan to distort and deceive, and yet I also pray I would never live in fear of his rage. You are greater by far, and I am Yours. Amen.

GRACE AND PEACE REFLECTION JOURNAL

- As you look at the list of the world's "usual suspects," which two compete most with God to be the source of your peace? (Circle any that apply to your circumstance.)

Wealth	Freedom
Morality	Delusion
Pleasure Highs	Fame (Recognition)
Power (Control)	Connectedness

- What forms of trust do you need to begin cultivating to overcome these empty temptations?

  1. _____
  2. _____
  3. _____

- When misdirected and distorted, which of your core cravings create the most friction in your life and family? (Circle any that apply to your circumstance.)

Security | Identity | Independence | Significance | Innocence

- What practical and tangible steps can you take to get your craving pointed in the right direction?

  1. _____
  2. _____
  3. _____

NOTES:

_____

_____

_____

_____

_____

_____

_____

_____

_____

_____

_____

_____

_____

_____

_____

_____

Chapter 10

HELPFUL ECHOES AND HAPPY SHADOWS

Imagine the year is 2031, and you are piloting the first solo mission to Mars. As you approach the famed red planet, you marvel at its tranquil beauty, the soft orange glow, the rusty contrast between its craters and plains, its mountains and canyons. Yours are the first human eyes to witness these marvels up close and personal. What treasure awaits discovery upon its mysterious surface?

Shortly after you enter the never-before-breached atmosphere, your sense of wonder turns into terror as multiple alarms begin to sound in sudden high-pitched bursts. Half the switchboard lights up in ominous synchronized flashes, and your shuttle shakes violently. Eight of your nine thrusters have failed, and the navigation computer has gone dark. You leap to the manual controls and strap yourself in. With only one operational thruster, you can do little more than slightly manipulate the angle of your chaotic descent. Certain death is imminent! Your teeth are bared in a desperate grimace, and perspiration streams down your cheeks as you plummet toward the surface of the unknown.

With bone-jarring force, you strike the Martian plain and are sent skipping like a stone, grinding uncontrollably across both sand and alien rock!

Finally, there is stillness and silence. At some point during the crash, you blacked out; but as consciousness slowly returns, you are amazed to realize you are still alive. Carefully unbuckling your safety harness, you heave your aching body from the seat and cautiously make your way toward the escape hatch. As the door opens, your survival suit is met by an icy blast of unearthly temperature: minus 150 degrees Fahrenheit! Your first step onto the frozen unfamiliar soil is not that of an intrepid explorer, but of a desperate survivor. You glance up to see two moons, and on the horizon, the rotating axis of the planet is slowly bringing the sun into view. It is the same sun you have always known, only more distant and cold. Suddenly, you are struck with a horrifying realization: you are marooned in a foreign and hostile environment! There is no food, no usable water, no suitable oxygen, nothing apart from that which now lies jumbled and broken within the wreckage of your ship. As the sun rises, it dawns on you that though you are here; you were made for another world.

MADE FOR ANOTHER WORLD

I sense there are times we do not fully grasp how far the human race fell in the Garden of Eden. It was not a mere blip on the human timeline, but a cataclysmic event, one that transformed the very ground under our feet into foreign, and even hostile, soil. Indeed, the only reason we can survive here is because of the emergency provisions granted to us by a good God. Thankfully, among our many blessings, we have been gifted with an internal navigation system, powered by the deepest cravings of our soul, and programmed to return us to the peace of our original coordinates.

In his fantastic book, *Mere Christianity*, C. S. Lewis shares a tremendous insight:

> *Creatures are not born with desires unless satisfaction for those desires exists. A baby feels hunger: well, there is such a thing as food. A duckling wants to swim: well, there is such a thing as water. We feel sexual desire: well, there is such a thing as sex. If I find in myself a desire which no experience in this world can satisfy, the most probable explanation is that I was made for another world. If none of my earthly pleasures satisfy it, that does not prove that the universe is a fraud. Probably earthly pleasures were never meant to satisfy it, but only to arouse it, to suggest the real thing. If that is so, I must take care, on the one hand, never to despise, or to be unthankful for, these earthly blessings, and on the other, never to mistake them for the something else of which they are only a kind of copy, or echo, or mirage.*

In this brilliant excerpt, we hear the trumpet blast of two vitally important truths. At first sounding, we are awakened to the realization that we are indeed made for another world. The place we currently reside is not our true home. Our inability to find contentment in worldly things is a clear indicator that our true home is located somewhere else, or more specifically, *in someone* else. Earthly treasures cannot satisfy our core cravings, nor were they intended to. God has placed eternity into the hearts of mankind, and it is to the eternal that we must return our gaze—toward the *real thing*.

GOD HAS PLACED ETERNITY INTO THE HEARTS OF MANKIND, AND IT IS TO THE ETERNAL THAT WE MUST RETURN OUR GAZE—TOWARD THE **REAL THING.**

As long as the human race persists in the pointless practice of feeding fleshly appetizers to hungry souls, of offering temporal provisions to our eternal cravings, we will continue to be caught in a continuum of dissatisfaction—even if we increase the rations. We must fully awaken to the realization that what we are craving is the fullness of peace found in connection with Christ alone. To this craving, only a banquet consisting of the Bread of Life (John 6:35) and Living Water (John 7:38) will grant lasting satisfaction.

Upon the second sounding, we hear a beautiful return echo. This happy return helps us understand that not every echo discovered in earthly pleasure is deceptive or fraudulent. In fact, these reverberations often serve a helpful and happy purpose. They grant us blessed awareness as to the nearness of the Source Himself.

HELPFUL AND HAPPY

I used to play hide-and-go-seek with my cousin as a child. During one game, I couldn't see his physical body, but thanks to a well-positioned light (well positioned for me at least), his shadow was cast across the wall behind him, and so I found him. Several years later, I played the same game with my children. They were just little and not particularly good at seeking, so I would choose a hiding place and purposefully leave obvious clues as to my location. I would climb under a bed and leave my feet jutting out, or I would hide in a closet and purposefully sneeze or cough. The celebration upon being found was always exciting.

Many have found God in precisely the same manner; the discovery was prefaced by hearing a heavenly echo or perceiving a divinely placed shadow. Indeed, the world is alive with helpful echoes and happy shadows, all employed to help us encounter our Heavenly Father.

I have made much of the fact that worldly things (a.k.a., echoes and shadows) cannot fully satisfy our core cravings; however, when viewed appropriately, they *do* aid in the discovery of He who cast the shadow and sounded the original call. This is why King David so triumphantly sang in Psalm 19:1–2,

> *The heavens declare the glory of God; the skies proclaim the work of his hands. Day after day they pour forth speech; night after night they reveal knowledge.*

And why Paul so fervently preached in Romans 1:20,

> *For since the creation of the world God's invisible qualities—his eternal power and divine nature—have been clearly seen, being understood from what has been made, so that people are without excuse.*

Truly, the echo and shadow of God flash all around us in creation, offering tantalizing testimony regarding the even greater reality of the Creator Himself. As distinct members of this creation, the aroma of God can even be perceived within our own human-to-human interactions. For example, within the promise of a healthy marriage covenant, we see a reflection of God's faithfulness toward us. In our sacrificial love for each other, we can identify the faint silhouette of God's greater love for the world. In loving our enemies, an even clearer silhouette takes shape. God calls us to these actions so we might reflect His goodness into the lives of the people around us. Human forgiveness, humility, perseverance, generosity, compassion, and sacrifice—all these are mere reflections, echoes that reverberate forth from the heart of our Savior. They are divine works of grace granted even among unbelievers, that we might be reminded as to God's original intent and design. How disappointing it is when we naïvely claim *ourselves* to be the source of these heavenly kindnesses.

All around us, in joyful plenty, leap helpful echoes and happy shadows; and as Lewis pointed out, we ought not to be too hasty in the pious dismissal of these blessings as something fraudulent. Truly, such benefits only morph into sinful deceptions when we promote them beyond their intended station, when we practice them outside of their intended purpose, or when we elevate the creation above the Creator.

Regrettably, this "echo worship" is prevalent in our confused and desperate world. Many continue to worship animals and trees, bowing and praying to the earth or the stars. While this form of idolatry has been *modernized* to better suit a contemporary way of thinking, at its core, it remains the same old worship of nature. In similar fashion, science, activism, politics, and distorted moralities have also morphed into religions for some people today, even demanding the tribute of worship and submission. Sadly, this trend seems to be growing in popularity. At the root of much of it, as always, is humanity's pitiful interest in controlling others and worshipping themselves.

We would do well to recognize these false religions and cults for what they are. Still, in our new awareness of worldly counterfeits, let us not rush to name everything a deception. In fact, Scripture teaches that we are to be people who *transmit* a heavenly echo and who *cast* our Father's shadow. Oh, that even in our own lives, the world would perceive the mighty reflection of God Himself. Not because we have become godlike, but because the light and testimony of Christ now looms large in our hearts, uncontainable, and bursting forth.

Jesus said in Matthew 5:16,

> *Let your light shine before others, that they may*
> *see your good deeds and glorify your Father in heaven.*

Our Heavenly Father gets the glory as *His* shadow is perceived within the illumination of God-honoring behaviors. To this end, our marriages, our workplaces, and our social relationships ought to be environments where we offer and preserve security, identity, independence, significance, and innocence—not with ourselves serving as the source of fulfillment, but serving as a reflection of Christ: the true Source, to the glory of His Name.

SERVING AS LIVING REFLECTIONS

If you position a mirror, or a piece of glass, to focus the reflection of the sun on a specific point, you can ignite a fire. It's amazing! Many survivalists have found much-needed warmth and comfort using this method. Similarly, when we reflect the provisions of Christ toward specific points in our lives, it can greatly ease the tension of day-to-day living in a fallen world. Not just for ourselves, but for others as well. We are not the sun; we are the glass.

Without question, reflecting security, identity, independence, significance, and innocence is the best recipe for a happy marriage, the most reliable strategy for successful child-rearing, and the prime equation to maximize professional and social collaborations. Still, it must always be understood that we are called to *reflect* the Source—we cannot *be* the source. I do not say this as a slight against any individual, but as an honest acknowledgment as to the healthy limits of our biological and spiritual designs.

If Romeo and Juliet had been better supported in their relationship; if the Montague and Capulet families had joined together to celebrate a happy fairytale wedding; if the beaming couple then raised healthy, beautiful children—they still would not have been able to satisfy each other's soul cravings. Why? Because even Romeo and Juliet were incomplete without their Maker.

With this in mind, I would speak an important message of caution to my fellow "hopeless romantics." The message is this: a marriage partner *cannot* fulfill the insatiable depth of your soul's craving. To place such an unreasonable expectation on a spouse (or on a friend) would be grave cruelty. To be frank, it would equate to a form of idolatry. Sadly, many people have made idols of their spouses, looking to their significant other to fulfill an innate longing only God Himself can truly satisfy. The predictable result is discontentment, disappointment, and disillusionment. Your spouse is a blessing from God—but they cannot *replace* God. The great power of marriage is found in a lifelong partnership with a *helpful reflector*. He reflects God to her, she reflects God to him, and together they pursue the Source of life and peace. This movement from *source* to *reflector* changes everything. It lightens the burden while simultaneously amplifying the effectiveness.

An FCH reflection should be present in our parenting as well. As a father, I lament that we commonly focus our parental efforts on providing security for our children, but we frequently neglect to foster healthy identities or to model the practice of safe independence. Sadly, in many homes, affection is performance-based, and accusation abounds. It is not surprising then that our children pursue significance by tearing others down or that they grow up to be combative and defensive regarding their innocence. Reflecting security is important, but it's not enough. Our children are souls, and these precious souls must be pointed toward their Maker. If *we* are looking for fulfillment in worldly things—our children will as well. More than enrollments into summer sports camps, or providing the benefit of pre-paid college tuition, our children need us to reflect the peace and provision of Christ into their lives. We can leave them no greater heritage than this.

A similar principle also applies to our careers. From the perspective of worldly benefit: if your employer experiences the reflection of the FCH in your work efforts, you will climb the corporate ladder faster than you can say *hooray*! Conversely, if your actions threaten the security, identity, independence, significance, or innocence of your company, you will soon find yourself looking for a new job. The way you manage your soul cravings in the workplace will dramatically impact your everyday life.

Even so, I would invite you to consider the even bigger picture: your coworkers are wandering *souls*! Your boss (apart from Christ) is a displaced *soul*! Each one of them has been wonderfully made in the image of God, and their only hope for fulfillment is in connection with Him. God has sent you into your workplace, your school, and your home as His reverberation, so … *reverberate*. Let them see the reflection of Christ in you.

The cravings of the world are tenacious and strong, and while you cannot personally *be* the fulfillment of that craving, you *can* reflect the bountiful provisions of Christ. Truly, the practice of reflecting the FCH in your everyday relationships will bring hope and stability to the lives of others and warmth to your own. This is what Jesus intended when he commanded us to love our neighbor as ourselves. It's what he meant when he said, "Let your light shine" (Matthew 5:16). In a nutshell, He is calling us to be helpful echoes and cast happy shadows. Why? So that the souls of those around us might better perceive their Maker and leap up in joyous recognition.

In the next chapter, we will delve into the details. Now that we better understand the *deep why* and the *deep what*, we will take the next step in implementing the *deep how*. We will pinpoint our current location, determine where we need to be, and strategize how to get there.

DEAR LORD,

THANK YOU, THAT YOU ARE A JEHOVAH JIREH, MY PROVIDER. YOU ARE THE SOURCE OF EVERYTHING I NEED. FORGIVE ME FOR ALL THE OTHER PLACES AND PEOPLE IN WHICH I HAVE SOUGHT YOUR PEACE. I HAVE MADE IDOLS OF THE VERY THINGS YOU INTENDED TO SERVE AS BLESSINGS. I CONFESS THIS, AND I THANK YOU FOR YOUR GENTLE MERCY. TEACH ME WHAT IT MEANS TO REFLECT YOUR LOVE AND HOPE INTO THE LIVES OF THOSE AROUND ME. I PRAY MY STORY WILL YIELD CLEAR TESTIMONY TO YOUR GOODNESS, FAITHFULNESS, AND TRANSFORMING POWER. THANK YOU FOR THIS BEAUTIFUL WORLD YOU'VE CREATED FOR US. GRANT ME THE GOOD SENSE TO RECOGNIZE YOUR LOVE, YOUR CREATIVITY, YOUR MAJESTY, AND YOUR ECHO AND SHADOW IN THE LIFE AND WONDER AROUND ME. AMEN.

ECHO AND SHADOW
REFLECTION JOURNAL

- What Divine blessings have you potentially elevated to idol status in your life?

  1. _____
  2. _____
  3. _____

- What can you do to correct the mistake of these unfortunate promotions? (Don't be vague. Consider practical steps and possibly even a timeline for the completion of these steps.)

  1. _____
  2. _____
  3. _____

- What helpful echoes and happy shadows did God employ to help you first perceive Him?

  1. _____
  2. _____
  3. _____

NOTES:

Chapter 11

WHY AND HOW?

Some years ago, I was driving down a stretch of highway between Edmonton and Calgary, Alberta. As golden fields of wheat and barley drifted by my window, I switched on the car radio and set the dial to a popular local talk show. The host, along with a selection of highly educated guests, were collectively attempting to solve the problem of youth crime. This issue had been widely reported in the media, and I was keenly interested in what they had to say about it.

The topic was relevant, the goal was noble, and the motives of the participants were sincere. Unfortunately, their worthy ambition was derailed from the very beginning. I remember the discussion well. They began by asking the right question: "*Why* are so many youth turning to crime?" I leaned forward, excited for a varied and spirited discussion to begin. It never materialized. Instead, the host simply answered his own question, emphatically stating, "We know the human race is born inherently good, so the problem is clearly environmental."

His panel of guests quickly agreed with him, and it was determined that no further exploration into the *why* was necessary. Little more than sixty seconds had passed, and they had already settled on a diagnosis, one that was woefully incomplete. The rest of the program was spent doling out prepackaged advice. Some of this advice made logical sense: limit youth access to violent video games, ensure that healthy lunches were available in schools, make certain that each academic campus had student counselors readily available, etc. Finally, they ended the program by encouraging their listeners to elect governing officials who would implement or mandate their solutions.

These proposals were not unreasonable, but they clearly did not address the deep root of the problem. Truthfully, they barely skimmed the surface. It should be noted that instances of youth crime were not reduced in that community.

> *(Side note: More recently, those governing officials have simply adjusted their definition of crime, thus creating the illusion of success.)*

As I consider the division, the confusion, and even the rage that is so prevalent in our world today, I often think back to that radio program. Having established a rushed and shallow diagnosis, the host and his panel of well-meaning guests were derailed before their "solution train" could gain any helpful momentum. Having misidentified the problem, a deep fracture appeared in the tracks, tipping their locomotive onto its side, where it lay helplessly in the dirt, pumping out steam.

If we are to effectively address the many challenges plaguing our society today, we will need to begin by *correctly* identifying the root of the problem. It is my hope that after considering the previous ten chapters, you now have a better understanding of the *deep why*: the cravings of the human soul that propel each of us through life and time. Still, just in case there is any remaining confusion, please allow me to summarize.

A SUMMARY OF THE HUMAN STORY

There *is* a God! To His glory, authority, power, and goodness, there is no end. From nothing, He created everything. He merely spoke, and the entire universe leaped into existence at the sound of His Voice. Planets and stars, solids and liquids. Both the visible and the invisible. Gravity, momentum, oxygen, gas—everything known and all things yet unknown. The great wonders of creation are beyond comprehension, and *we* (yes, you and I) are identified among them. In fact, we are the crown jewel of this miracle, having been created in the image of God Himself. This privilege is uniquely gifted to the human race. We alone bear His likeness, even being granted the joy of calling Him our Father. Magnificently, we are the beneficiaries of His greatest affection, and as such, God has shaped us for the highest and most beautiful of purposes, namely, to experience the joy of knowing Him and the delight of being known *by* Him.

Like an eagle gliding through the wide sky above, or a power cord plugged into a power outlet, our souls have been similarly designed to find both their joy and their strength in the heart of our Heavenly Father. This Great Heart is the mold from which we have been cast, and the realm of His magnanimous presence is the eternal expanse in which we are freely released to explore, imagine, laugh, and love. What a delight!

Sadly, this is where our human story takes its tragic turn. At a pivotal stage near our earliest inception, we chose to reject our

Creator—to flee from His loving presence! In so doing, mankind joined Satan and his minions as the only creatures foolish enough to despise the good purpose of their creation.

Just think of it—earthworms and eagles did not rebel against their Maker! The sun happily radiates just as God designed it to, and it will continue to do so until God says otherwise. Even icky spiders and rodents did not sink low enough to reject the purpose of their creation! We alone pursue the mad folly of abhorring divine design! Some might argue that our unique actions are the result of our higher intelligence, but I ask you, do our actions warrant the smug claim of higher intelligence? Our forebears began it, making the cataclysmic decision to go their own way, fueled by the nefarious hope of eclipsing God and redefining their own existence.

To reject one's purpose and design is not easy to do. It requires an extensive rending … making it a messy affair. Not surprisingly, we did not make a clean getaway. We left tainted and marred by the tempter, that serpent who originally inspired us toward our woeful decision in the Garden of Eden. The poison of his lies sunk deep, infecting our hearts and distorting the souls of each new generation. This inherited infection is called the sin nature. We are born with it, and as we grow up, we each begin to *willfully* feed and nourish it. I cannot merely assign all blame to my ancestors, nor even to the serpent. The consequence of sin is now my own, and the consequences are real.

In true self-deprecating fashion, the sin nature works relentlessly to divert our soul cravings away from the fulfillment of their Creator and back toward the frustration of corrupted creation. One by one, these cravings are destructively deflected and sent reeling off course—from the infallible toward the fallible, from the authentic toward the forgery, and from the promise toward the curse. This misdirection is the root cause of all our pain and disappointment, as it leaves us in a state of perpetual unfulfillment. Such is the fallen human condition.

Praise the Lord, God has never given up on us. Instead, He has moved to repair the tear through the work of Jesus Christ. Motivated by an unimaginable love, the Immortal One chose to die on the cross to pay the penalty for our sins. Essentially, He stepped in front of the bullet we unwittingly shot at ourselves. Such is His passion for us.

Even more relentless than the sin nature is God Himself. He continually seeks to restore and redeem—to draw our souls back to the home of His heart. The pull of His magnetic heart is felt even by those who do not yet revere Him. And for those who call on His Name? He offers to save completely!

One might presume this to be the end of our problems. After all, if "God is for us, then who can be against us?" (Romans 8:31). The answer, sadly, is ourselves. We alone stand in our way. Through the most self-deprecating of all follies yet, many have chosen to reject God's offer of restoration. Our modern society is, even now, attempting to expel God from His own creation. While previous generations were guilty of distorting God's Word and blaspheming His Name, recent generations now attempt to deny His very existence. Like madmen claiming to be enlightened, we confidently strut toward our own doom.

Removing God is like biting the only hand that can truly feed us; it's like a drought-laden field cursing a soft summer rain. Thankfully, expelling the Divine is not within our power. Still, hundreds of millions now claim to be irreligious; though truthfully, they have simply imagined a new religion, one that positions themselves to be god. This "god" hates the same people they hate and loves the same things they love, but ultimately, he or she is powerless to provide, restore, or save. Truly, our situation is dire, but what can we do about it? How can we get our souls back on track?

THE ANSWER AND THE ELEPHANT

In our early years of marriage, my wife chose to homeschool our children through their elementary years. They would often begin the day by reading aloud from the famed devotional publication *Our Daily Bread.* My wife would then ask the children questions regarding what they had just heard, and my ten-year-old son would generally respond with the same predictable answer, "Ummmm, the answer is Jesus." This happened every day.

Sometimes he said it to be funny (as it made his sister giggle), while other times, he said it playfully, to get under his mother's skin (as only he could). No matter what the question was, he would reply with the same pat answer. Not surprisingly, he was generally right! Jesus *is* the answer! However, there is an important nuance to be highlighted here: knowing Jesus to be the answer is completely different from knowing Jesus ... who is the answer! Do you see the difference?

One knowledge is academic; the other is relational. One is religiously traditional, while the other is holistically transformational. The discrepancy between these two understandings is the difference between despair and hope, knowledge and faith, disappointment and fulfillment. As we previously learned, Jesus alone is the solution to the cravings of our souls. Only He can satisfy.

That said, let's acknowledge the elephant in the room: many Christians live unfulfilled lives! There, I said it. But why is this true? If Jesus is the answer, why isn't the answer working? Why are so many Christians stuck in the same endless cycle of anxiety and fruitless ambition as the rest of the world?

ROCK AND SAND

Answering the question of Christian unfulfillment is not complicated, though it is a delicate matter, as it could potentially tread rather aggressively on our sense of innocence. In a sense, I suppose this is my "trigger warning" regarding the next few pages. As we explore the answer, try your best to evaluate yourself honestly— not for the purpose of condemnation, but in the interests of true growth and solution. There is one thing we can be certain of: the problem does not lie with God, but with ourselves. James 1:5–8 declares,

> *If any of you lacks wisdom, you should ask God, who gives generously to all without finding fault, and it will be given to you. But when you ask, you must believe and not doubt, because the one who doubts is like a wave of the sea, blown and tossed by the wind. That person should not expect to receive anything from the Lord. Such a person is double-minded and unstable in all they do.*

In this passage, James exposes the problem of double-mindedness. He warns us that a double-minded person will not experience peace and fulfillment from the Lord. In fact, their lives will be marked with instability—the *opposite* of peace. Such a person asks God for wisdom, but when God grants them their request, they second-guess Him. Essentially, they set themselves up to be the judges and editors of biblical truth and spiritual insight. God reveals to them the Source of Light and Life, but they determine instead to seek alternative or additional sources. Perhaps that is not what they set out to do originally; nonetheless, that is the result. If God's wisdom sounds contrary to what they *want* to hear, they reject or revise it. Sadly, this is not an uncommon scenario, even within the Church. The apostle Paul addresses a similar problem in 2 Timothy 4:3, as does Jude 1:3–4.

Many love the idea of Jesus the Savior, but they recoil at the thought of Jesus as Lord. They lean in when they hear the message of eternal life in Christ, but they squirm when the pastor talks about "taking up our cross and following Jesus." This half love for the gospel has led many to attempt to live half-Christian lives, lives that are half-yielded to the Spirit and which only express half agreement with biblical teaching. Rather than building our houses upon the Rock (as Jesus encourages in Matthew 7:24), we choose instead to build our homes adjacent to the Rock. Therein lies the root of the problem: with only one foot on the Rock and the other on the sand, instability is inherent and inevitable.

> THEREIN LIES THE ROOT OF THE PROBLEM: WITH ONLY ONE FOOT ON THE ROCK AND THE OTHER ON THE SAND, INSTABILITY IS INHERENT AND INEVITABLE.

This tainted form of belief can sneak up on any of us, which is why the apostle Paul gave us clear instructions to regularly "examine yourselves to see if you are in the faith" (2 Corinthians 13:5). I routinely perform these self-assessments and frequently must address the disappointing results. Still, avoiding these important evaluations generally results in dangerous personal blind spots.

This epidemic of double-mindedness has produced many individuals who now imagine they can believe *in* God without actually *believing God.* Somehow, they claim to believe in His *work*—but they are unenthused about His *Word.* They look to the

Bible as a source of comfort—but they increasingly marginalize its authority in their lives.

Jesus laments this trend toward half belief in Matthew 7:22–23, where He predicts a future throng of people standing before Him and *claiming* to have believed in Him, and yet He will send them away because he never knew them. What a devastating outcome! If only they had been honest with themselves about their beliefs. Maybe then they could've adjusted course; maybe then, they could've legitimized their relationship.

Without question, half faith will in no way result in peace and fulfillment for the soul. The best it can produce is a brittle imitation peace for the here and now but nothing in the long run.

THE DEEP HOW

So how do we solve the problem of Christian unfulfillment? How do we make the peace promised in the scriptures and celebrated in the songs our living reality? In a sense, all your previous reading has led you to this pivotal moment of revelation! (Cue drum roll.)

The *how* can be summed up in two words: *truly believe!* Take God at His Word! Trust Him … *fully!* Place your security, identity, independence, significance, and innocence in the hands of Jesus. Not symbolically or metaphorically, but truly and completely. This is what we have been designed for! This is the true secret to success.

We must identify and root out our half beliefs and partial surrenders, presenting them to God to be refined and made whole. Why? Because perfect peace will *only* be experienced on the day we

1. fully *believe God* and
2. choose to rest on the firm foundation of His unfailing Word.

Before you throw this book across the room in disgust, believing this answer to be cliché and annoyingly predictable, let me explain. Believing God, and resting on His Word, is precisely what Adam and Eve *stopped* doing the very moment they listened to the serpent's lies. They chose to believe Satan's narrative over the truth of the Living Word. It is no coincidence then that it is back to this original point of divergence that we are called to return, reestablishing our faith connection with God. The Holy Spirit desires to right this ancient wrong and reunite each of us with the Maker of our souls. When this divine bond is secure, there is no medical diagnosis, no crime wave, no recession, and no scandal that can diminish your hope. But without this connection, even our assurances are volatile and uncertain.

Perfect peace is realized within our Heavenly Father's embrace—and *only* within our Heavenly Father's embrace. The entire weight of Scripture draws us toward this cliché, yet life-changing, diagnosis and prescription.

Truly believe God! This is the answer we've been searching for! Or is it? Does it seem … underwhelming? Were you expecting (or maybe even hoping) for something more complex and grandiose? Perhaps that's because we've forgotten what belief is! We've thought about it in such an ambiguous way for so long that we no longer recognize its true nature. Belief in God is the greatest force a human soul can possibly wield. It can move mountains, soften hardened hearts, conquer kingdoms, shut the mouths of lions, and save fallen souls. It has even been known to raise the dead. And yes, it alone can deliver authentic, unshakable peace, even when everything around us is falling apart. True belief is the answer!

But someone might ask, "What am I supposed to 'believe in' specifically?" For starters, believe in the power of Christ's death and resurrection. Believe in His *complete* forgiveness for those who repent of their sins. Believe in His victory over the grave—and the *radical* implications that has for your life. Believe in the unfailing nature of His Word. Believe that God is supreme in power and authority and that He will eventually judge the world through a perfect balance of justice and mercy. Believe Him when He tells you that your life here on earth is not all there is, that a great and glorious eternity is coming—which means you don't have to live in servitude to earthly ambitions or fears.

Fully believe God's Word. This is the secret to fulfillment. This is the point of rest toward which you are being drawn.

Isaiah 26:3–4 (NLT) praises God, singing,

> *You will keep in perfect peace all who trust in you, all whose thoughts are fixed on you! Trust in the LORD always, for the LORD GOD is the eternal Rock.*

Please note who the beneficiary of perfect peace is: *those whose thoughts are fixed upon God.* This is why Satan's primary point of attack is your mind! The enemy of our souls seeks to disrupt our happy reunion by distorting our thinking and distracting our attention. He works to spark argument, controversy, and doubt by continuing to recite his tiring old line, "Did God really say …" (Genesis 3:1). The world is now filled with these deceptions and clever manipulations. In such a faithless environment, we would do well to repeatedly echo the prayer of Mark 9:24: "I do believe; help me overcome my unbelief!"

The man who originally prayed this prayer was humble enough to recognize that his faith was lacking—that it needed to grow. It should be noted that Jesus performed a miracle in response to his confession. Oh, that we would also exercise the humility of honest self-awareness.

Peace for the soul will require us to grow in our faith, and growing in our faith will require the deliberate intent to do so. The next chapter will delve deeper into the fundamental process of belief and trust. It's a chapter designed to facilitate understanding, healing, and spiritual growth.

DEAR LORD,

I HAVE DISCOVERED THE PRESENCE OF HALF FAITH IN MY LIFE. I LONG TO TRUST YOU FULLY, BUT SUCH TRUST CALLS ME TO A MEASURE OF SURRENDER THAT MAKES ME UNCOMFORTABLE. I CONFESS THIS LORD, AND I ASK YOU TO BEGIN A GREAT WORK WITHIN ME. I HAVE BEEN DOUBLE-MINDED, AND I ASK FOR THE GRACE OF YOUR DELIVERANCE. TEACH ME TO SAY NO TO THE SERPENT'S PROCLIVITIES AND YES TO YOUR PROMISES. YOUR WORD PROMISES TO GIVE WISDOM TO THOSE WHO SINCERELY ASK FOR IT. **I ASK FOR IT, LORD.** HELP ME TO RECEIVE IT BY FAITH, AND TO TAKE MY STAND UPON ITS FIRM FOUNDATION. AMEN.

TRUE BELIEF REFLECTION JOURNAL

- Write a comparative list of things you find easy to trust God with versus the things you struggle to trust God with.

  Easy to Trust   Hard to Trust
  1.   1.
  2.   2 .
  3.   3.
  4.   4.

- What do your lists tell you about where you're at in your faith journey?

- God has not left you alone on this journey. What do you need to begin praying for?
  1. _____
  2. _____
  3. _____

NOTES:

_____
_____
_____
_____
_____
_____
_____
_____
_____
_____
_____
_____
_____
_____
_____
_____
_____
_____

Chapter 12

THE LONG MIRACLE

Most of us are familiar with the old idiom, "You can lead a horse to water, but you can't make it drink." As someone who has owned horses, I can verify the truth of this statement. Many years ago, I worked as a horse trainer. During the summer of 1995, I hauled a trailer load of my best stock from eastern Alberta to southern Oregon. It was a journey of over 900 miles, and I had planned several stops along the way where I could water the horses. I specifically recall one young colt who refused to drink. He was thirsty—that much was obvious—but he was overstimulated, and he would not to put his nose in the water trough. I stood and waited for him. I patted his neck and spoke softly, hoping to soothe his equine anxieties. I splashed my hand in the water to draw his attention. Then I waited, splashed, whispered encouragement, and did it all over again. Eventually, I tried pulling his head down toward the water—a move he fiercely resisted. It was frustrating. I cared about him, but he simply would not drink. As a result, I spent much of the journey worrying about his condition. I repeatedly led that horse to water, but no matter how hard I tried, I could not make him drink.

For most people, this proverb has a less literal meaning. Generally, it means you can give someone an opportunity, but you can't force them to make the most of that opportunity. The same is true of our souls. We can (and should) communicate to one another the blessing and benefit of growing in faith … but we can't *make* anyone grow in faith. When you truly care for someone, their refusal to "drink" can be very discouraging. You desperately want the best for them, but they won't accept it.

I have experienced this same frustration in my professional life. I *know* trusting God will dramatically improve the lives of the people I am privileged to counsel, but I can't *make* anyone trust Him. At times, I've wanted to blurt out, "Just believe God!" but of course, that's a fruitless strategy (and an oversimplification).

In order to grow in peace, you *will* have to grow in faith, but rather than simply urging you to *believe harder,* I prefer to try a different tactic—a more constructive and effective one. I'd like to share with you four insights that I believe will *help* you grow in faith, and there, discover the peace you are looking for.

SANCTIFICATION (INSIGHT #1)

If any of you have ever experienced a compound fracture, you know it's important to reset the bone and cast it as quickly as possible. You also know that certain aspects of this procedure can be excruciatingly painful and debilitating. Nonetheless, it's a *necessary* process, and it's performed in the best interests of your overall health and well-being.

The same is true of a rotten tooth. Even with modern anesthetic, drilling out the rot, or pulling out the tooth entirely, can be extremely uncomfortable. But once again, we submit to this process because it's *necessary* for our overall health.

Sanctification is a word Scripture uses to describe having our souls reshaped, refined, and strengthened by the Holy Spirit. It, likewise, "removes the rot" of distrust or "sets the bone" of broken belief, and it places us on the path toward greater faith and fulfillment.

Sanctification grows, matures, and enriches us. Still, like rehabbing a broken bone or visiting the dentist's office, sanctification can be uncomfortable, but we purposefully engage in it for the sake of our overall health.

This crucial process is central to the development of deeper faith. I often refer to sanctification as *the long miracle*. That is to say, it's the miraculous work of the Holy Spirit that heals, purifies, and grows us over time. Unfortunately, we live in a culture today that demands immediate gratification. We develop technologies and launch streaming services, all to fulfill the ever-increasing demand for prompt service. Not surprisingly, it's never enough.

This same demand for immediacy has crept into our expectations of God. Even the most conservative of Christians prefer to experience an instantaneous miracle, and at times, God grants us this grace. I've seen it—I've even experienced it. But more often, God prefers to work through the *long miracle*. Why? For the very reason that it requires dedication, engagement, personal sacrifice, and persistent surrender. While immediate gratification is never satisfied and invariably keeps asking, "What have you done for me lately?" the experience of journeying with the Holy Spirit through the *long miracle* of sanctification matures, strengthens, and purifies us—yielding a superior result. As your first step toward deeper faith, I encourage you to submit to the process of sanctification once again. Always remain open to the possibility of an immediate miracle, but embrace the *long miracle* for the good and beautiful gift it is. Nothing grows your connection with God faster than traveling with Him through challenging times. Sanctification creates this precise opportunity.

COLLABORATION (INSIGHT #2)

While sanctification is generally associated with being set apart for spiritual growth and benefit, the *process* of sanctification is heavily focused on the physiological. As human beings, we comprise three primary elements: body, mind, and soul. As long as we are living here on earth, these elements remain woven together and interconnected. Encourage or abuse one of them, and the other two will feel the effect. This is important information to grasp. It's a truth that many seem to have overlooked. Sanctification will engage you, body, mind, and soul. For as long as our time on earth lasts, we are the collaboration of these three elements. This is our basic human makeup, and it has profound implications for every aspect of our lives.

Consider this: God became flesh through the incarnation for the *very purpose* of empathizing with us in this frailty, and any talk of faith, belief, or sanctification must *also* consider this ever-present reality. Not surprisingly, God's Word does exactly that. The scriptures consistently include directives for the body and mind, even when the primary goal is spiritual growth. Romans 12:1–2 calls us to offer our *bodies* as living sacrifices and to be transformed by the renewing of our *minds*. Hebrews 13:1 reminds us to fix our *thoughts* on Jesus. This type of phrasing reverberates throughout the entire Bible. Clearly, sanctification demands an "all-hands-on-deck" approach.

You are a collaboration of three parts: two parts mortal and one part immortal. This collaboration has unique benefits while simultaneously posing significant challenges. Jesus referenced these challenges in the garden of Gethsemane, lamenting of His sleeping disciples, "The spirit is willing, but the flesh is weak" (Matthew 26:41).

I have spoken at length about the destructive influence of the sin nature, and yet growing in faith will additionally require us to contend with our own, literal, "weak flesh."

WEAK FLESH (INSIGHT #3)

Many have fairly wondered why growing in faith can be so difficult. It seems we can listen to countless sermons on the great love and power of God yet remain unchanged. We can experience lofty spiritual moments—being moved to tears and confession—yet within days, hours, or even minutes, we once again experience the same old fears and anxieties. Why is that?

One reason might be our failure to funnel these experiences into the process of sanctification, whereby they can be tested, verified, and affirmed. Another reason might simply be that we haven't realized how tremendously weak our flesh actually is. The comment Jesus made in the garden of Gethsemane regarding *weak flesh* was not mere hyperbole but factually true.

Scientific studies of the human brain have revealed that habitual thinking can create grooves in our neural network, circuits that access and transfer information at faster speeds each time the pattern is repeated. Similar to continually driving on the same road or walking on the same path, if you *think* in a specific direction often enough, it will form a rut (of sorts) in your brain. This is why an angry, bitter, or suspicious person can't "just stop" thinking angry, bitter, or suspicious thoughts upon request. Trenches have formed in their neural network—aqueducts that instinctually direct thoughts in a specific direction. This is not an insignificant obstacle to overcome, and it has profound implications for our faith journey.

Sadly, our neural pathways have shuttled error back and forth for so long that deep and debilitating grooves are now cut into our daily thought patterns. This makes implementing changes to our belief system difficult. We often struggle to adjust our opinions about things as trivial as paint color, so how much more difficult will it be to overhaul our entire perspective regarding existential truth? In many cases, these grooves have not just formed over years, but over *generations*. This compels me to ask some important questions of myself:

- What are *my* habitual thoughts?
- What direction does my thinking most often trend?
- What ruts have been forming in *my* brain?

Are they ruts of faith or ruts of fear? Ruts of divine trust or of self-reliance? Is my mind being shaped by God's Word—or by worldly propagandas? These are important questions to ponder, especially in our modern age. Our smartphones, tablets, computers, TVs, and even our watches, are *constantly* flooding our minds with persuasive content to process: content that either enhances our propensity toward biblical faith or counteracts it.

And of course, we haven't even broached the subject of brain/body chemicals and hormones; they, too, wield profound influence. Is there any hope for meaningful change amid all our biological weakness?

The answer is *yes*—but it's not a flippant *yes*; it's a *thoughtful yes*. It's a *yes* that recognizes our need for physical healing and the literal reshaping of our minds. This is something for which we must urgently pray. Perhaps you will receive this healing through an instantaneous miracle, but more often, God will call you toward the *long miracle*. He'll invite you into the "trenches" with Him, where you can survey the damage firsthand and work Side-by-side to repair it.

Let me emphatically state that there *is* hope! In addition to Jesus being a miracle worker, those same scientific studies have proven that neural pathways *can* be repaired and rewired. A new way of thinking *can* replace the old way, and helpful grooves can replace unhelpful ones. This reshaping will require God's grace in association with a willing spirit, determination, and accountability. It will require the engagement of God's Word, the power of the Holy Spirit, and the support of godly friends and counselors. This is another important step in growing your faith.

ACCOUNTABILITY (INSIGHT #4)

Sanctification is not a *do-it-yourself* project! Between our weak flesh and the sin nature, it is not difficult to be drawn off course, to suspend the divine process and begin sniffing around old counterfeits again. This does not mean that we *completely* walk away from the Lord but that we attempt to employ Him for worldly purposes. We expect (or even demand) God to satisfy the cravings of our souls using the *same* failed methods the world uses. We don't pray for faith; we pray for more stuff, stubbornly presuming that peace will be discovered therein. In other words, we stop looking to God as the Source of *new* life, and begin viewing Him as a new source for the old life—a celestial sugar daddy of sorts. This type of wild reasoning develops when we claim to have "found God," but we don't submit to sanctification and discipleship.

In this unfortunate scenario, our neural grooves remain relatively unchanged from their pre-salvation pattern, and the sin nature merely exchanges dark robes for white robes to better blend into a Christian environment. The apostle Paul warned of this in 2 Corinthians 11:14, saying, "For Satan himself masquerades as an angel of light."

Left on our own, we struggle to perceive these deceptions. But surrounded by godly brothers and sisters in Christ, we are better able to stay on course. With this in mind, I will *again* remind you that sanctification is not a do-it-yourself project. Besides God's Word and the Holy Spirit, I encourage you to invite fellow believers into the process. They will warn you of approaching danger, encourage you when you grow weary, challenge you when you drift toward ungodly thought patterns, and help pick you up when you stumble and fall. Accountability will be a true game changer in your pursuit of deeper faith. This is the very reason the Bible calls us to fellowship and discipleship.

THE TRANSFER OF POWER

The *purpose* of sanctification could easily be described as *the transfer of power*. It's the process through which we exchange our righteousness for God's righteousness, our accomplishments for God's accomplishments, our delusions for God's reality, and our weakness for God's strength.

Earlier, I quoted King David from Psalm 20:7:

> *Some trust in chariots and some in horses,*
> *but we trust in the name of the LORD our God.*

If we are to have any hope of experiencing true and lasting peace, we will need to shift our trust from "chariots and horses" to "the Lord our God." That's where the power is! We must also desist in our attempts to "live on bread alone" and prioritize more and more "every word that comes from the mouth of God" (Matthew 4:4). This shift is an absolute necessity!

However, as you attempt to execute these transfers, you can expect to be met with both spiritual and neurobiological opposition. That is to say, your sin nature will leap to defend its lies, and your neural network will yield the right-of-way to old habits. These opponents can be defeated through the *long miracle* of sanctification and through the support of godly friends who kindly share the burden.

In Philippians 4:8–9, the apostle Paul inspires us, saying,

> *Finally, brothers and sisters, whatever is true, whatever is noble, whatever is right, whatever is pure, whatever is lovely, whatever is admirable—if anything is excellent or praiseworthy—think about such things.*

He then ends the passage by presenting the benefit of such thinking, "And the God of peace will be with you."

Within these verses, we hear the apostle Paul imploring us to change the direction of our thinking. This is a vital step in our sanctification process: the development of new grooves.

As long as we are looking for fulfillment in worldly people, places, and things, we will remain discontent and unsatisfied. As long as we are shackled by half belief and double-mindedness, we will remain disillusioned and unstable. By God's grace, we must embrace sanctification, thereby growing in faith, trust, hope, and peace.

Taking into consideration our long history of *thinking in the wrong direction*, this exercise will initially prove challenging. The hard truth of the matter is that many of us have become addicted to the quick and destructive high offered by counterfeits and lies. Not only this, but our immediate gratification culture has spawned a pervasive disinterest in practicing spiritual and mental disciplines.

For the sake of effective strategizing, sometimes it's helpful to view ourselves as recovering addicts, confessing our addiction to worldly means and methods. We acknowledge our proclivity toward them, even while admitting they are empty and destructive. We embrace God, the highest of all powers. We commit to the process of recovery, and we surround ourselves with accountability partners, sponsors, and like-minded friends.

While the temptation for counterfeit highs may never fully dissipate (not until we reach Heaven), they become far easier to resist when we employ the right tools and surround ourselves with the right influencers. Always remember, your biggest sponsor and ally is God Himself. Yes, the sin nature is relentless, but God is more so.

Hopefully, these fresh insights will help you better understand your personal sanctification process. They will teach you how to pray, how to empathize with others, and how to develop peace sustaining faith.

DEAR LORD,

I THANK YOU FOR THE CLARITY OF YOUR WORD. I COME BEFORE YOU TODAY AND SURRENDER MY MIND. AT LEAST, I **WANT** TO SURRENDER IT. PLEASE HELP ME DO THIS, LORD. I PRAY THAT YOU WOULD HEAL MY BROKEN NEURAL PATHWAYS. DEVELOP WITHIN ME A GROWING SENSE OF TRUST. LORD, I'M STUCK. I NEED A MOTIVATOR. I NEED INSPIRATION. I NEED A MIRACLE! THANK YOU FOR BEING THE GOD OF MIRACLES. I NOW REALIZE THAT PEACE FOR MY SOUL CAN ONLY BE EXPERIENCED BY BEING WHOLLY YOURS. HELP ME TO WHOLLY TRUST, TO THOROUGHLY SURRENDER, AND TO FULLY EMBRACE YOUR GOODNESS AND POWER. TODAY, ON THIS DATE_____, I BEGIN A WHOLE NEW JOURNEY OF FAITH. I NO LONGER VIEW FAITH AS AN AMBIGUOUS FORCE, BUT AS AN INTENTIONAL CHOOSING OF LIFE. I CHOOSE TO TRUST YOU AFRESH. AMEN.

SANCTIFICATION REFLECTION JOURNAL

- What unhealthy ways of thinking have you adopted? In other words, what unhelpful ruts have been forming in your brain? (Examples may include negativity, fear, covetousness, skepticism, self-reliance, or others.)

  1. _____
  2. _____
  3. _____

- As your brain goes through a re-wiring/sanctification process, which godly friends or counselors can you invite into the process to add the benefit of holy accountability? (Choose those who will encourage and love you enough to speak truth to your particular counterfeit addictions.)

  1. _____
  2. _____
  3. _____

- A life of following and trusting God is the ultimate thrill for the soul. What adventures would you like the Lord to take you on? (Yes, it's OK to ask Him.)

  1. _____
  2. _____
  3. _____

NOTES:

_____

_____

_____

_____

_____

_____

_____

_____

_____

_____

_____

_____

_____

_____

_____

_____

_____

_____

Chapter 13

HOW TO SAVE THE WORLD

How beautiful are the feet of those who bring good news!
ROMANS 10:15

When distorted by the sin nature, the cravings of our souls become cruel taskmasters, forever demanding relentless pursuit while offering no lasting reward. Many promises are made from sources incapable of making a delivery. This is the plight of humanity—the loop in which the entire world is helplessly caught. We are like hamsters, running eighty years on a stationary wheel and getting nowhere.

Understanding each other in this way can inspire us toward compassion and self-awareness. When we awaken to the fact that individuals with control issues are likely struggling with fears relating to security or significance, or rebellious young people with distortions of identity or independence, or defensive friends with the burden of innocence, when we understand *the deep why*, we are empowered to respond differently than we would otherwise.

Perhaps with compassion instead of disgust. Perhaps with patience in the place of rushed abandonment. Perhaps with a heavenly solution rather than worldly condemnation. Moreover, when we finally recognize the people around us for what they are: *eternal souls* created in the image of God, temporarily encased in mortal bodies, afflicted by the sin nature, and desperately trying to find peace … and *not* simply as disagreeable biological creatures—well, that changes everything. This truer understanding grants us the opportunity to become better spouses, better neighbors, better parents, and better witnesses to God's goodness.

Now that we've received a proper diagnosis, we are afforded the opportunity to become part of the solution, rather than part of the problem.

My hope is that this fresh understanding of the human soul will bring clarity to specifics in your life, in addition to sparking a transformative awareness as to the unconscious motivations of those with whom you share this planet. Realistically, the best a book can do is impart information; it is left to us to employ the information wisely.

Security—Identity—Independence— Significance—Innocence

This is what you are looking for in your spouse and what your spouse is looking for in you. It's what you were hoping to find when you chose your career, and it's what your employer is looking to discover within your labors. That said, we must always remember that true satisfaction can *only* be realized in connection with our Maker. There is no substitute for our God! It is His heart toward which our souls are drawn. The best gift we can give one another is to faithfully reflect *Him*.

Throughout the ages, philosophers and songwriters, even beauty pageant contestants, have all dreamed of a utopia: the realization of world peace, a place of harmony and contentment. Every political party predictably campaigns on the same promise and forever underperforms. Even the sincerest delivery attempts fail as the searcher, the dreamer, and the legislator all forage for solution in counterfeit sources.

Still undeterred, humanity has set off across the globe in dogged pursuit of our greatest treasure. We began our quest equipped with little more than a walking stick. Eventually, we learned how to ride a horse. Soon the wagon was invented and then the ship. Suddenly, great oceans could be traversed, and entirely new continents explored. All the while, we've been thinking, "If we explore, we will grow in experience and prosperity. If we accumulate enough knowledge and property, surely we will find what we've been looking for amongst all our stuff."

The canoe and the steam locomotive, the automobile, the airplane, and the space shuttle—all these advancements serve one unconscious purpose: to help us move faster and farther in our relentless pursuit of something that, should we ever catch it, would deliver us the ultimate reward: PEACE. That at least is what the subconscious mind tells itself. And yet our ever-increasing speed and ease of travel do little to help, as we generally end up looking for satisfaction in all the wrong places: in creation rather than the Creator.

Despite unprecedented prosperity, comfort, and freedom, the world has not become a happier place. Perhaps you've noticed that it is now the world's richest citizens who are leading the current space race. They possess everything the earth has to offer, but it doesn't equate to peace, so they reach in desperation for the stars. They have claimed their efforts are for the benefit of humanity as a whole, and while I do not doubt their good intentions, I note that satisfaction for *our* souls doesn't exist there either. The answer to our craving is both closer and farther away than most have thus far imagined.

Speaking of the fallen world, Romans 3:17 laments,

> *The way of peace they do not know.*

And Isaiah 53:6:

> *We all, like sheep, have gone astray,*
> *each of us has turned to our own way.*

And so the world launches off in hot and high-intensity pursuits (in the wrong directions) when all the while, peace has been held out—offered freely to all in Christ Jesus. Ultimately, *this* is the message that saves the world, to the degree that it is willing to be saved: the message *of total provision in Christ.* He is the answer for our hungry souls!

Contrary to the promises of many well-intentioned (yet misguided) Christian leaders, this provision of peace is *not* free—it will cost you both your hamster wheel and your Rock-adjacent lifestyle. And due to the effects of a self-deprecating sin nature, letting go of hamster wheels and sandy living might be harder than you first imagine. Sadly, our rabid addiction to counterfeits runs deep. Thankfully, the love and passion of Christ runs even deeper.

The Caveat

There is a caveat here that must be acknowledged. The peace found in Christ Jesus must be declared, but more than that, it must be *modeled*. This is where the gospel message meets its greatest challenge. Too many of us are living in the shadow of the Summit, stuck at base camp, anxiously pitching our tent on the promises of God without ever walking in the peace of truly *knowing* God. Our relationship with Him is judicial, but not intimate; it's theologically sound, but not living; it's grace-filled, but not peace-filled. To this incomplete testimony, the world will offer little response. A revival in our nation ought to begin with a revival in the Church, and a revival in the Church must begin with a revival in our hearts. In anticipation of this holy awakening, I urge you to join me in ceaseless prayer.

It is the *exhibition of peace* in the life of the believer that most effectively inspires the skeptic to sit up and take notice. This peace is the tangible evidence of living faith. By all means, *tell* people about Jesus; but in a world where most have heard it all before, an authentic *modeling* of peace will persuade in a way no argument can. To this end, we must take our shoes of faith off the boot rack of stationary theology and begin walking in them, running in them, even dancing in them—not just for the sake of a watching world, but for our own joy. Good theology *must* be preached, but it must also be *lived*. The apostle Paul reminds us of this gospel intent in 1 Corinthians 4:20, declaring, "The kingdom of God is not a matter of talk but of power."

Our actions must match our words, for this is the faith modeled to us in the scriptures. In addition to many miracles, our biblical mentors experienced beatings, threats, imprisonment, rejection, shipwrecks, persecution, and even execution, *yet the power of peace prevailed*. They believed God in the face of it all, and that is the reason, in large part, why the gospel has been preserved for us today. Less is not required of us!

Before I begin evaluating the counterfeits plaguing my neighbor, I need to take stock of my own life. I urge you to take what you are learning about yourself and about your God and head for the Summit. That is where peace resides, in the cleft of the Rock. It is not *stories* of the mountaintop that will motivate others to join us, but the sight of us *on* the mountaintop. Surrender your hamster wheel, pack your tent, grab your climbing gear, step onto the Rock, and let's go.

THIS IS US

Adam and Eve hung all their hopes on the supposed life-giving properties of an apple, as propagated to them by the serpent. Since that original blunder, mankind has made very little deviation. Though now our "apples" take the form of bank accounts, careers, politicians, relationships, and even sexual freedoms, all of them are counterfeits, frauds, and illusions that cannot deliver satisfaction.

It has been said that "misery loves company," and this is definitely true of Satan. He longs for us to share in his despair. This is an important truth for us to apprehend. The Devil is not enjoying a life of carnal sin (as some movies depict). Rather, he's angry, bitter, broken, and lashing out. His invitation is not one to communal fulfillment but to multiplied emptiness.

As you move forward in the healthy pursuit of your God-given cravings, if you listen carefully, you will hear the soft slither of your sin nature keeping pace, ever seeking to distort, discourage, and misdirect. The serpent is a liar and a deceiver, pedaling his own worthless oils. I counsel you to crush his head in Jesus's Name. Submit him to Christ to be nailed to the cross. May the boots of our faith be made of snakeskin.

SECURITY—IDENTITY—INDEPENDENCE— SIGNIFICANCE—INNOCENCE

As much as an unedited family portrait or selfie, these five cravings capture the core pursuits of the human race. They are a picture of our hope and our desperation simultaneously. In addition to being the "mega goal" of human pursuit, peace is also a fruit of the Spirit, and all throughout the scriptures, we discover that peace is the natural and abundant by-product of truly *knowing* Jesus. Coming to know Jesus in this manner will require that we follow Him, study Him, talk to Him, listen to Him, believe Him, and generally spend time with Him. He is the source of fulfillment you crave! Anchor yourself to Him, test the connection, practice the connection, then model the connection. You will experience no greater joy and shine no brighter light than this. It is God's will for you to find peace in Him who is the Prince of Peace!

AN INVITATION

At this point, I would invite you to spend a moment in self-reflection. Perhaps you began this book primarily interested in learning more about your deeper self, and you have unexpectedly discovered God on every page. Thank you for continuing to read; and I hope, if nothing else, that you *have* learned more about your soul, in addition to now understanding why Christians believe what they believe.

While it is theoretically possible to ignore the "religious portions" of this book and still feel enriched through a deeper understanding of the soul, I would encourage you to continue investigating the person of Christ. You could further this investigation by reading the Gospels of John and Luke, then the books of Acts,

Romans, Philippians, and Colossians, followed by the rest of the New Testament. I suggest you begin with a modern translation, the NIV or the NKJV (or something similar). I would additionally encourage you to visit a Bible-believing church, where you are sure to meet other fallible people, all reliant on the grace of God and purposefully assembled, in order that they might encourage one another toward the peace of knowing God.

Or perhaps you're already a believer, but you now possess a deeper awareness of your need for God's provision. Maybe you have sensed a shallowing to your faith (or you're experiencing the monotony of base camp), and you long to pursue God to new heights and with a fresh dedication. I would give you the same advice as above and inform you that God is equally excited at the possibility of a deeper connection.

The heart of God is magnetic, and regardless of our current level of faith, the Sovereign of the universe longs to draw us even closer to Himself, increasingly filling us with an abundant provision of security, identity, independence, significance, and innocence.

A Salvation Prayer

Dear Lord,

I have grown uncomfortably aware of the presence of sin in my life. I have tried to hide and excuse it for so long. Father, I now confess this sin, and I ask for your forgiveness—I cry out to You for mercy. Grant me the strength and the willingness to turn away from vanity and pride and toward the security and the hope of Your unfailing Word. I thank You, Jesus, not only for coming to save my soul but also for bringing me abundant and eternal life. I cling to You as my Savior, and I desire to follow You as my Shepherd and Lord. I now receive Your provision of salvation and grace, and I excitedly pursue Your provision of peace. Lord, I believe! Please reveal and eradicate any remaining unbelief. Amen.

A PERSONAL LETTER TO GOD:

Dear Lord,

_____

_____

_____

_____

_____

_____

_____

_____

_____

_____

_____

_____

_____

_____

_____

_____

_____

_____

_____

_____

_____

_____

_____

_____

_____

Chapter 14

UNDERSTANDING PERSECUTION

For the time will come when people will not put up with sound doctrine. Instead, to suit their own desires, they will gather around them a great number of teachers to say what their itching ears want to hear. They will turn their ears away from the truth and turn aside to myths. But you, keep your head in all situations, endure hardship, do the work of an evangelist, discharge all the duties of your ministry.

2 TIMOTHY 4:3–5

The title of this chapter may sound out of place, but I assure you it isn't. I have written this book with the intent of introducing you to your soul, and by extension, introducing you to the souls of those around you. I have sought to lead you on a journey—one that culminates in practical instructions for abundant living. It's my hope that you now possess a greater understanding of both yourself and the world around you. This chapter will further that understanding through a unique and timely crescendo. We'll begin with a brief historical review.

FIRE AND BLOOD

Despite its often-savage notoriety, Rome was actually an extremely tolerant society. The Caesars had long since discovered that maintaining order in an empire increasingly populated by *conquered* peoples could only be managed by granting its diverse citizenry the right to practice their independent faiths and traditions. As I mentioned earlier, if autonomy is infringed upon too heavily, a revolution will be imminent. No nation can thrive in an atmosphere of perpetual upheaval, so as long as the citizens paid their taxes and didn't get *too* loud, Rome granted freedom of worship and belief to all. This resulted in Roman culture becoming a vast melting pot of ethnicity and diversity.

Included in this melting pot, yet distinct, was a rapidly increasing number of individuals practicing the *new* religion of Christianity. At the time, it was considered to be a religion for the marginalized, as it was the destitute and the less fortunate who were turning to Christ en masse. Christianity did not differentiate between rich and poor, male and female, slave or free. It taught equality, mercy, forgiveness, and future glory. Hope was extended to all, without favoritism, and with no thought to prior social standing. Understandably, this held great appeal for those who had been relegated to the periphery of society for generations.

Additionally, the Christians were known for the passionate worship of their God and for their staunch rejection of all other gods. They were bold, celebratory, and evangelistic. In a world where almost everyone rooted their identity in the religion of their fathers, the Christians brought the idea of religious conversion to a whole new level. This bend toward monotheism and evangelism irritated many people, and this irritation came to a climax on the fateful night of July 18, AD 64. The "how it happened" is still debated; regardless, somehow, in the middle of the night, a fire broke out in the merchant quarters of Rome. Fanned by the summer breeze, it soon became a raging inferno, spreading death and destruction for six days and seven nights. By the time the flames were subdued, 70 percent of the great city had been burned to the ground.

In the aftermath of the tragedy, frustrated by hurt and loss, the people looked for someone to blame. With eyes full of suspicion, they directed their gaze toward Nero, the emperor. Nero was an eccentric, arrogant man, and he had often made plain his discontent with the city, widely boasting of a desire to rebuild Rome and rename it after himself. Knowing the citizens now suspected him of malfeasance, and fearing for his life, Nero desperately needed a scapegoat, someone toward whom he could redirect the building rage. He quickly made his fateful decision—he would blame the Christians. Nero made the argument that because the Christians *insisted* there was only one God, and because they were so bent on conversion, they had angered all the other gods, heaping guilt and condemnation upon everyone.

According to the Roman historian Tacitus, the official charge leveled against them was "hatred against mankind." And so the word went out. "The Christians hate us! They don't respect our preferences, and they don't respect us. They have brought guilt and consequence down upon everyone! They are responsible for the devastation!" This declaration led to the first widespread persecution of the Christians, including atrocities so terrible they are difficult to even fathom.

I do not recount the above story simply to reminisce about a sad chapter in our history but to issue a serious warning as to the gathering storm I see looming on the horizon. Indeed, even now, we witness the groundwork of persecution being laid. Hatred against mankind! That was the charge made against them, and this will soon be the charge leveled against us.

THE ROCK AND THE HARD PLACE

As Christians, we understand that our faith is rooted in love. We know Galatians 5:6, "The only thing that counts is faith expressing itself through love." And the royal law described in James 2:8 to "love your neighbor as yourself."

The entire Christian faith is founded upon God's amazing love for us; we respond with a reciprocal love for Him—which then overflows into a love for one another. Indeed, even in this modern hour, the world greatly benefits from our acts of Christian kindness: compassion for the poor; mercy and forgiveness; love, love, and more love. The world, however (because of the effects of a distorted craving), perceives something *completely* different. When we say, "gospel of hope," they hear, "outdated rules." When we say, "Savior," they hear, "You're not good enough as you are." And to a certain degree, they are not fully mistaken.

For thousands of years, Christianity has held to the same fundamental truth—namely, that we are *all* sinners, and we *all* need Jesus! Again, the message of the gospel does not differentiate or show favoritism between persons, and therein lies the modern-day resentment. The Good News of Jesus Christ *assumes* we already possess an awareness regarding the bad news of our fallen selves. Unfortunately, culture today has been cleverly blinded to themselves (by Lil' Miss Indignant), and they are vehemently offended at the suggestion of any wrongdoing. They crave innocence, but the Good News of Christ unabashedly infers universal guilt. This is an inference that the modern world cannot tolerate. In their minds, Christianity, by default, makes people feel bad about themselves (particularly when it comes to sex and sexuality), and it, therefore, needs to be relegated to the trash bin of history. This relegation will eventually result in persecution, and the justification for this persecution will be an accusation akin to "hatred against mankind."

While the unbelieving world's assessment of Christianity is both unfair and verifiably untrue, it is historically consistent with its pattern and progression throughout time. If the liberation movements of the '60s and '70s were about establishing a fresh tone of *independence* and the tech boom of the '80s and '90s a new sense of *security* and *significance*, the 2000s have thus far been focused on grooming self-righteous forms of *identity* and *innocence*. Indeed, our current irreligious culture is wholesale bent on expunging guilt by declaring its *own* truth and evangelizing its *own* perceptions of reality. This culmination of counterfeits has created an environment that is increasingly hostile to the Christian faith, and it places today's believers between a Rock and a hard place. The *Rock* is the Rock of Ages (whose message we are sent to faithfully live and declare). The *hard place* is the hard heart of modern culture, which has grown tired of listening to our bibliocentric chatter. Caught in this troublesome pincer, we are pressed, but not crushed! It *will* lead to persecution, but God will never abandon His people.

DESPERATE MEASURES

You may be reading this and saying, "Wait, stop! I don't want to be caught in a pincer! I want to believe in Jesus, but I don't want to be accused of hatred and intolerance! Can't we just preach and live the gospel in a way that doesn't offend anyone? Isn't that a reasonable solution?"

Many Christians are understandably asking this desperate question, but realistically, honestly, the short answer is *no*! Preaching the gospel without offending is *not possible*. Even Jesus couldn't do it, and He warned us in John 15:20, saying,

> *If they persecuted me, they will persecute you also.*

And Paul, in 2 Timothy 3:12:

> *In fact, everyone who wants to live a godly life in Christ Jesus will be persecuted.*

The grudge the world holds against the believer today is regarding our undying belief in the authority and infallibility of God's Word. This belief is not something we can modify or edit, for in doing so, we would cease to be true believers. That, of course, is the intended goal of both the serpent and an increasingly offended world: to silence the truth, control, and even end biblical belief.

The Gospel of Jesus gracefully presents true reality, *including* the reality of our fallen selves. To omit this crucial segment of reality would be no different from telling half-truths, and we have special names for those who purposefully tell half-truths: liars and deceivers! Additionally, by sharing the Good News of Jesus *without* referencing the bad news of ourselves, we effectively make the Good News pointless. After all, if I'm not a sinner, I don't need saving!

To the ears of Lil' Miss Indignant, the true gospel *always* sounds offensive. The problem is not with the Rock; it's with the hard place.

We, of course can—and should—learn the art of speaking in a fashion that is not unnecessarily accusatory or inflammatory. Truly, this simple adjustment would benefit all our relationships. Ultimately, however, God's message of salvation clearly infers that redemption is both *necessary* and *exclusive* to the Christian faith. Modern culture will eventually sniff out this inference and take offense, and there is little we can do about it.

CLOSING WORDS

In addition to sharing the message of God's unimaginable love for us (and the provisions for life found only in Him), we must also continue to identify the problem of sin, declaring the necessity of both faith and repentance—or it's not Christianity.

I cautioned earlier never to underestimate the expansive influence of our craving for innocence. It was the first humanity Adam sought to reestablish after the Fall, and its distortion is a primary cause for the friction we see in our culture today. When someone says or does something that triggers a sense of guilt (in this context, the gospel message triggering the unbeliever), the sin nature activates an immediate fight-or-flight response ... and the world is done avoiding us!

Whether you believe this to be a prophetic word or simply the logical conclusion in consideration of the facts, I will state my belief definitively: just as the first wave of persecution brought the unjust accusations of hate and intolerance, so also will the next.

What we desperately need is a movement of the Spirit, sent to waken the slumbering soul, soften the hardened heart, and open both blind eyes and deaf ears. To this end, He is already working; and to this end, I continue to pray. Amen.

DEAR LORD,

I THANK YOU FOR THE HOPE FILLED MESSAGE OF PEACE FOR THE SOUL. EMBOLDEN US TO SPEAK BOTH THE TRUTH OF OUR FALLEN CONDITION, AND THE GLORY OF YOUR ABUNDANT PROVISION TO THE WORLD AROUND US. SADLY, LORD, OUR PROBLEMS OF UNFULFILLMENT AND DISCOURAGEMENT ARE NOT JUST PERSONAL OR GEOGRAPHICAL; THEY ARE GENERATIONAL AND WORLDWIDE— EVEN RESOUNDING THROUGHOUT THE AGES. HEAVENLY FATHER, I PRAY FOR A GREAT AWAKENING. I PLEAD FOR A HOLY REVIVAL TO SWEEP THE LAND. AN AMELIORATION THAT CELEBRATES YOUR GRACE AND EMBRACES YOUR PEACE. I PRAY FOR REIGNITED SOULS, FOR IRON TO BE DRAWN TO THE MAGNET OF YOUR HEART ON A SCALE NEVER BEFORE WITNESSED. ALLOW US TO BE PART OF THIS LORD; IN FACT, LET IT BEGIN WITH US. AMEN.

Action Items

Considering the nature of this book, it seemed appropriate to dedicate a few pages to action items. I have listed six that I believe will help get you to where you need to be. Additionally, I have left blank spaces so you can add some of your own.

1. RECOGNIZE THE CRAVINGS OF YOUR SOUL FOR WHAT THEY ARE.

Security, identity, independence, significance, and innocence. These cravings are the *deep why*, the source of your every motivation. God placed these cravings in your soul to help navigate a great spiritual migration, one designed to draw you toward the safe harbor of a relationship with Him. No matter how far we may wander, we are each gifted with this internal compass. These cravings cannot be satisfied in any earthly noun; rather, they demand fulfillment in God Himself. This is an existential reality that must be actively acknowledged, or we will remain in danger of deception and perpetual unfulfillment.

2. RECOGNIZE YOUR SIN NATURE FOR WHAT IT IS.

The sin nature relentlessly seeks to divert our God-given cravings away from God and toward empty and fallible sources. It began in the Garden of Eden, and it continues to this very day. Much of the world around you has chosen a tragic and debilitating deception, so don't be fooled or confused when hearing them loudly champion fraudulent sources of fulfillment. I encourage you to actively identify and avoid these counterfeit solutions. Hopefully, you are now better equipped to do so. These counterfeits are generally not difficult to recognize; they point to the creation rather than the Creator, to personal preference and selfish ambition rather than divine purpose and design. Additionally, you can expect Mr. Despair or Lil' Miss Indignant to show up on your doorstep at some point. I pray you recognize them for the distortions they are and expel them in Jesus's Name.

3. IN ADDITION TO EXPERIENCING PEACE *WITH* GOD, I ENCOURAGE YOU TO ACTIVELY PURSUE PEACE *IN* GOD.

While God's grace is our primary need, peace for our souls remains our highest want. God, in His goodness, graciously offers provision for both our need and our want. In light of this, I urge you to consider the summit of Mount de Paz. Don't forever camp at the judicial level of relationship with God but press on toward the joyful heights of a full trust relationship. When this connection is secure, there is no medical diagnosis, no crime wave, and no recession or scandal that can diminish your hope. The Sovereign of the universe is yours, and you are His. Security, identity, independence, significance, and innocence, all are realized within our Heavenly Father's embrace—and *only* within our Heavenly Father's embrace. Actively pursue this heightened connection.

4. BELIEVE GOD!

This is the *deep how*! Belief in God is the most powerful force a human being can possibly wield, as it holds power over both the physical and the spiritual realms. If God says it, you can believe it—*fully*! Be honest with yourself and beware of practicing a "pre-rooster faith": a faith that believes it is deeper than it actually is. You can actively grow your faith by diligently spending time in God's Word, through regular conversation with the Lord, and by surrounding yourself with people who are nearer to where you want to be. We are daily bombarded with propaganda that encourages us to believe *the serpent*; therefore, we must purposefully encourage one another toward trusting our Maker. Truthfully, many of us have become counterfeit addicts. In response to this fact, it is crucial that we invite healthy influencers and accountability partners into our lives. Always remember, sanctification is not a do-it-yourself project.

5. REFLECT GOD!

Be a helpful echo! Be a happy shadow! While you must not, and *cannot*, be the source of the FCH for anyone else, you can and *should* reflect the provisions of Christ. Your spouse, family, and friends all need this reflection in their lives. Reflecting the provisions of Christ is exactly what the Scripture means when it calls us to love our neighbors— and even our enemies. Jesus Himself is the Light of the world, so "letting your light shine" (Matthew 5:16) is specifically referencing the act of reflecting Christ who is in you. Jesus has sent you on this illuminating mission! Pursuing this Heavenly call will bring light and stability to the lives of others, as well as warmth and purpose to your own.

6. PRAY FOR STRENGTH AND DISCERNMENT!

The serpent is a clever deceiver, meaning his counterfeits aren't merely generic but custom-made for each one of us. He knows exactly what forgeries best suit our individual tastes, and it is these he will present. In addition to knowing God, it is important we understand ourselves, for it is these two pearls of wisdom in tandem that will deploy our impenetrable defense. The entire purpose of this book has been to help you toward this holistic awareness. Still, book knowledge is not enough; you will need the strength and discernment of the Holy Spirit. God is willing to grant you this provision, but you must receive it and actively walk in it.

7. CONSIDER SPREADING THE WORD.

If this book has been a valued source of information or encouragement to you, please consider how you can help get its content into the hands of others. Is there a friend, a family member, or even a stranger whom you feel would benefit by awakening to the reality of their core humanities? If so, please consider lending them your copy of this book. Or better yet, help connect them with their own copy. With all the emptiness "going viral" in the world today, it would be wonderful to begin spreading something constructive. Even now, the magnetic heart of God is drawing each one of us to Himself. As more of us begin *responding* to this divine connection, our relationships will improve, our communities will be transformed, and the world as we know it will change for the better. Changed lives change lives! Thank you for taking part in this holy awakening.

8.

9.

10.

GRATITUDE AND DEDICATION

ALL GLORY TO GOD, WHOSE MERCY AND MAJESTY HAVE BLESSED ME WITH UNENDING REASONS TO PRAISE HIM.

SPECIAL THANKS TO MY LOVING WIFE, WHO HAS PERSONALLY SACRIFICED SO MUCH IN RELEASING ME TO COUNTLESS HOURS OF STUDY, REFLECTION, AND THE PORING OVER OF PAGES. SECOND ONLY TO JESUS, SHE IS MY MUSE AND INSPIRATION.

TO MY CHILDREN, OF WHOM I AM SO PROUD, AND WHO HAVE FAITHFULLY SERVED AS MUCH-NEEDED "CHRIST REFLECTORS" TO THEIR FALLIBLE EARTHLY FATHER.

TO MY PARENTS, WHO, ABOVE ALL OTHER THINGS, TAUGHT ME THAT GOD IS REAL—AND THAT HE'S WORTH KNOWING.

Post-Credit Scenes

SCENE ONE

He blinked his eyes slowly, painfully, grimacing as the sunlight flashed unobstructed throughout the room. Consciousness was slowly returning. He was lying on his back, struggling to focus his eyes on the blurry expanse above him. His head was throbbing, and his memory seemed filled with a strange haze. As his vision slowly cleared, he noticed a small brown stain on the corner of a white ceiling tile overhead. He stared at it intently. Yes, the stain was shaped like a palm tree. Funny, it reminded him of a specific palm that grew by the main pool at the Empress resort in Honolulu. The tree had a strange dog-leg-shaped kink just below the first set of branches, and he had often wondered why the resort hadn't removed it, replacing it with something more fitting an establishment that charged $1,100 a night. This stain looked just like it—it was uncanny.

Slowly, his eyes drifted toward the source of the uncomfortably bright light: a large picture window that filled nearly the entire wall. The curtains were wide open, and the sun was streaming in. *Why are the curtains open?* he thought to himself irritably.

His mouth felt dry and chalky. Sensing a strange pressure in his arm, he glanced down and was surprised to discover a series of hoses inserted into his wrist. He was in the hospital! The unusual odor he had pondered since first waking up now made perfect sense—a unique blend of old flowers and sterilization. Why was he in a hospital bed? Someone had dressed him in a flimsy patient gown, but he could see his clothes folded neatly on the shelf beside the window: his gray pants, leather belt … *and his blue shirt.*

All at once, his memory came rushing back. He remembered the rooftop … *and the ledge* … the twinkle of human life bustling below him! He remembered the despair … *and losing his balance*! Someone had shouted, and as he began to fall, he had felt a great yank at the back of his shirt collar. He had no memory as to what had taken place after that.

There was a stir of movement beside him, and slowly, painfully, he turned his head. His wife was curled up, asleep on an orange plastic chair. The blanket that had no doubt been wrapped around her shoulders was now half on the floor. He stared at her in disbelief and was immediately flooded with emotion. Her clothes were wrinkled and disheveled. Clearly, she had been waiting beside him for some time. Even as he stared, her eyes opened and connected with his. They each caught their breath!

He remembered the very first time she had taken his breath away. Years earlier, he had swung by his old alma mater to pick up a friend and had unexpectedly met her in the parking lot. She was struggling to unload a box of books from a cart into her car, and he had stopped to help. They struck up a casual conversation and laughed as they swapped conspiracy theories regarding the dean's personal parking space. That brief moment together was all it took—*she was the one,* and he knew it. After returning home that day, he immediately received a phone call from his friend—whom he had forgotten to pick up.

Ever since that chance meeting in the parking lot, he had never really cared about spending time with anyone else. It was just her. That is how he *felt*, but in recent years, it wasn't what he had communicated to her.

Now here, in the hospital room, almost seventeen years later, they once again surveyed each other with nervous eyes. So much had happened; so much trust had been violated, and so much water had flowed under the bridge!

Neither of them spoke. Both were uncertain of what to say, and each was afraid of what might happen when the silence was broken.

Suddenly, he was struck by a shocking wave of embarrassment and shame. He thought of all the years he had wasted chasing empty promises, all the times he had taken this precious lady for granted in the pursuit of his own selfish desires. And of course, there was a growing sense of humiliation as to the reason he was now laying in a hospital bed. All the years of pain and disappointment now rushed upon him with incredible weight and clarity. He had never cried in front of her before. In fact, he had never cried in front of *anyone* before, not since he was very small! From early childhood, his burly father had taught him that "Real men don't cry in front of people." Nonetheless, through the tension of it all, the tears suddenly rushed upon him unexpectedly, and he blurted out with a sob, "I'm so sorry!" Unintentionally, he almost shouted the words.

Dropping the blanket, she rushed toward him, carefully pulling his head to her chest. Her own tears flowed, and they both just cried, their mingled tears communicating a depth of feeling that words had so long failed to convey. Caught up in this healing moment, time passed without awareness. At one point, a nurse came into the room, but sensing the importance of what was taking place, she quietly retreated, softly closing the door behind her.

Finally, he again whispered, "I'm so sorry!"

For a moment she was silent, then, through a voice thick with emotion, she replied, "I don't want to go back to the way things were! I don't want to feel alone and unseen!" She paused, struggling with her words, "But I want you to know that I love you … and I want to work through this … together."

He held her close, afraid to let go. They could hear muffled voices speaking intermittently over the hospital intercom and the rumble of carts rolling back and forth in the hallway, but they were distant sounds. Their focus was solely on each other in this moment.

"There's something else," she said, sitting up so she could look at him directly. "A lot has happened. I'm … different than I was before."

She wiped the tears from his cheek, biting her lip as she worked to formulate her words. "I'm a Christian now. I've been … I'm not the same person anymore."

A Christian! Her words brought back the faded memory of his grandfather. He had been a kindly old man, always with a sparkle in his eye and candy in his pocket. He remembered him sitting in that big brown chair with the flowery fabric and reading from an absurdly large Bible. As a small child, he had often wondered about that big book, but his grandfather had died when he was very young, and the memory had died with him.

Tenderly, his wife cradled his face in her hands. Speaking softly, nervously, she asked, "Can I tell you about it?"

Her eyes eagerly searched his face, and he smiled back at her in a way she hadn't seen in years. "Please do," he replied.

SCENE TWO

Big Tony took one final drag on his cigarette before flicking the remains to the sidewalk. He pressed the fading embers into the concrete with the toe of his enormous shoe and briefly considered his next move. It was 11:45 p.m., but light was still streaming through the windows of the old stone building.

Ever since Reverend John McDermott had accepted the call to pastor Living Hope Community Church, the lights had never gone out. The church doors remained unlocked twenty-four-seven and, with his small parsonage attached to the main church building, Reverend John made himself readily available to anyone seeking spiritual guidance or prayer. Most folks were happy to pray or reflect alone in the sanctuary, but they always knew Reverend John would be there in their moment of need.

All this was information Big Tony knew nothing about, and he wouldn't have cared even if he *had* known. In fact, Big Tony hadn't darkened the door of a church since he was eleven years old. Back then, he only attended for the purpose of snaking cash from the offering basket as it passed by. Still, Margaret had spoken of this place several times in recent weeks, and if she was hiding somewhere, he suspected it might be here.

Big Tony strode toward the entryway and quietly stepped through the front door. Soft lighting sufficiently illuminated the room and, sure enough, there sat Margaret, three rows from the front. She was alone, her head bowed in apparent prayer. Unquestionably, she was an attractive woman, and Mr. Gabriel would be thrilled when he returned her to him.

Big Tony permitted himself a brief moment of satisfaction at the completion of a successful investigation, then he moved forward and sat down beside her. She appeared small and helpless next to his intimidating frame.

"I'm here to take you back, Margaret," he said flatly.

He had expected her to negotiate or even to run. Margaret did neither. Instead, she said something that caught him completely off guard.

"Big Tony, do you know that you are dearly loved?"

If someone had suddenly stepped forward and slapped him across the face, he wouldn't have been more surprised. Her question momentarily shocked him into silence. He glanced nervously around the room, as if suspecting a trap.

Margaret continued, "In fact, you are loved *so* much that someone died to make you safe—and whole."

Big Tony touched his tongue to his lip in a nervous twitch. "What are you talking about, Margaret?" He stood up, stepping away to survey her more carefully. "Are you drunk?" he asked, peering into her eyes to assess for intoxication.

Margaret laughed, looking back at her giant associate with amused eyes. "You've always known how to make me laugh, Big Tony. No, I'm not drunk." She patted the seat beside her. "Sit back down."

Big Tony remained wary. He grabbed a chair from an adjacent row, spun it around and straddled it, keeping the back of the chair between himself and Margaret—almost in a defensive posture.

"Are you happy?" she asked.

Once again, Big Tony wasn't prepared for the question.

"What?" He was bewildered. "Am I happy? What kind of question is that? I'm not hungry—if that's what you mean."

Margaret giggled. "No, that's not what I mean." She turned her body to face her captor more directly. "I've discovered something recently that I think you should know about." She paused for a moment, gathering her thoughts. "We aren't alone in this world, Tony—and we never have been. There's a God in Heaven who cares for us. In fact, he cares so much that he died on a cross to pay the penalty for our sins. *All* of our sins, Tony, and for you and me—that's a whole lotta sin. We've made some pretty bad choices."

Margaret thoughtfully rubbed the needle scars dotting the inside of her left arm before continuing. "But God doesn't just want to forgive us; he wants to bring peace to our souls. He wants to redeem our lives. He wants us to *know* him—can you believe that, Tony?" As Margaret spoke, her excitement and intensity level grew. Despite himself, Big Tony was listening intently. Her words sounded foreign—even out of place and fanciful—but somehow, he found himself wanting to hear more.

"I don't know about you," Margaret reflected, "but I didn't have caring parents. They allowed things to happen to me that never should've happened. But God isn't like that. No matter what anyone else does, God wants to be a good dad to us. He wants to heal us. He wants to help us. He wants to teach us and be our friend. Isn't that amazing?" This time Margaret paused, waiting for Big Tony to answer.

"Well ..." He awkwardly cleared his throat, grappling for a response. "That all sounds good, Margaret, but if God is so good, why is the world so dark and filled with trouble?"

Margaret stared at Big Tony in amazement. He seemed sincere. She rose to her feet. With Tony still seated, she could look him straight in the eye ... or she *almost* could.

"I won't pretend to have all the answers," she replied, "but I do know that, if we're honest, we need to own a lot of this darkness and trouble for ourselves. God is the solution—he's never been the problem."

Margaret suddenly had an idea. She grabbed Big Tony's giant hand and pulled him to his feet. "Follow me," she said excitedly. Before he knew it, he was lumbering along behind her like a bull being led by a chickadee. They paused outside a brown door located to the left of the church platform, and Margaret knocked. She glanced up at him with contagious anticipation, still holding his hand. They could hear a soft rustle of movement inside, then the door opened, revealing a small gray-haired man in striped pajamas.

"Oh, good evening, Margaret," the man said, smiling. As he spoke, a cheerful lady in a housecoat appeared behind him with an equally large smile.

"Good evening, Mr. and Mrs. McDermott," Margaret beamed. "Sorry to bother you so late, but my friend and I have some questions about Jesus."

"Well, you're in luck," Pastor John replied enthusiastically. "He's our favorite topic."

Mrs. McDermott clapped her hands joyously. "I'll put some tea on," she announced happily, already disappearing down the hall and making the turn toward the kitchen.

"I'll help you, Mrs. McDermott." Margaret released Big Tony's hand and raced after her.

Having been abandoned by the ladies in the entryway, the two men surveyed each other carefully. This evening had not at all gone the way Big Tony had expected. He was accustomed to having people look at him with awe—and *fear*—but Pastor John looked at him with warmth, kindness, and genuine welcome.

"I'm happy you've come to visit us, son. We've been praying for you for a while now." Pastor John's tender words pierced Big Tony's rough exterior, and something deep within him began to melt.

"I'm happy to be here, sir," he said softly. "I *do* have a lot of questions." Big Tony ducked his head as he entered through the doorway of Pastor John's home.

If anyone had been observing from the street that night, they would've witnessed four figures huddled around a humble dining room table, talking, praying, and discovering life in abundance.

About the Author
AN INTERVIEW BY RAYMOND REED

From a tattered canvas tent staked on the grass beside a remote lake in British Columbia, Canada, to a log cabin perched high above the clouds in the majestic Rocky Mountains, Cory Rosenke spent much of his childhood in the debilitating grip of poverty, isolation, and even homelessness.

"I found my reprieve in exploration," Cory explained during an interview in January 2023. "As a kid, I would wander the lonely mountain slopes with a walking stick, a book, and my faithful dog. When I found a vantage point that suited my tastes, I would lean against a tree, open my book, and experience the magic of being whisked away into faraway lands and varied perspectives."

Many of the books that captivated his curious mind were not your typical *young readers*. At the ages of eleven and twelve, Cory was eagerly exploring *Laws* and *Republic* by Plato, *Ethics* by Aristotle, and *Meditations* by Marcus Aurelius. "I especially loved, *Where I Lived, and What I Lived for,* by Henry David Thoreau," says Cory, "as it seemed to meet me where I was at." His early teen years found him exploring a new province (Alberta) and embarking on new literary adventures: the diverse works of Sigmund Freud, Edmund Burke, Plutarch, and C. S. Lewis, just to name a few.

"I'm not exactly sure what sparked it all," Cory said in response to my inquiry, "but from a very early age I wanted to understand why people did the things they did. I especially longed to understand myself. For as long as I can remember, I've yearned to identify the deeper why lurking beneath the surface why. Eventually, I found Jesus, and the puzzle pieces finally began to fit together."

Cory Rosenke's insatiable curiosity has remained a constant force throughout the ups and downs of living. From a cowboy to a carpenter; a business owner to a small-town pastor; a seminary graduate to a dynamic multi-national teacher, Cory Rosenke's varied and eclectic life has graced him with a unique and insightful perspective—an innovative voice that pierces the fog of false religion and philosophic dogma.

Now an accomplished author, theologian, and pastor, Cory remains as inquisitive as ever. He currently resides in the San Francisco Bay Area of California (as of 2023), and he spends his days as he always has—reading, writing, exploring, shepherding, and forever watching and wondering.

A free ebook edition is available with the purchase of this book.

To claim your free ebook edition:

1. Visit MorganJamesBOGO.com
2. Sign your name CLEARLY in the space
3. Complete the form and submit a photo of the entire copyright page
4. You or your friend can download the ebook to your preferred device

Print & Digital Together Forever.

Snap a photo

Free ebook

Read anywhere